PETER'S ALMANAC

BOOKS BY LAURENCE J. PETER

PETER'S ALMANAC
PETER'S PEOPLE
PETER'S QUOTATIONS
THE PETER PLAN
INDIVIDUAL INSTRUCTION
CLASSROOM INSTRUCTION
THERAPEUTIC INSTRUCTION
TEACHER EDUCATION
THE PETER PRESCRIPTION
THE PETER PRINCIPLE (_WITH RAYMOND HULL_)
PRESCRIPTIVE TEACHING

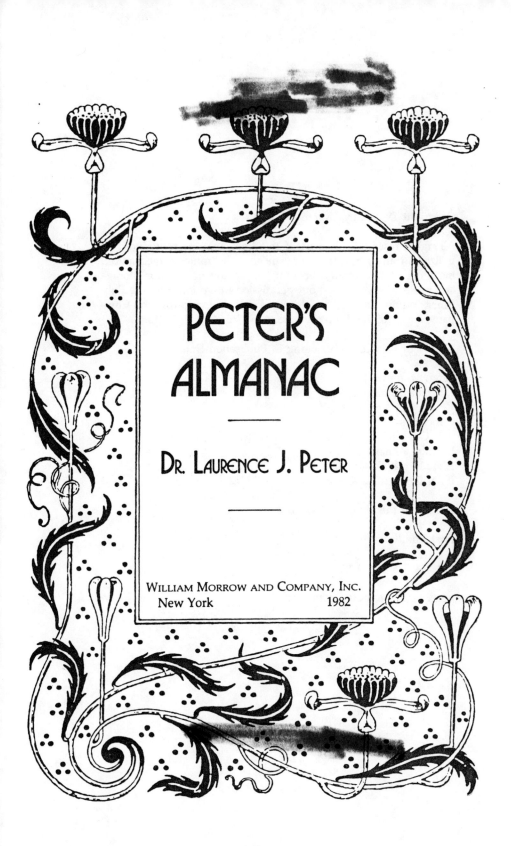

PETER'S ALMANAC

Dr. Laurence J. Peter

William Morrow and Company, Inc.
New York   1982

Library of Congress Cataloging in Publication Data

Peter, Laurence J.
  Peter's Almanac.

  Includes index.
  1. Gift-books (Annuals, etc.)   I. Title.
II. Title: Almanac.
AY12.P4   1982   031'.02   82-8031
ISBN 0-688-01612-X   AACR2

Printed in the United States of America

First Edition

1 2 3 4 5 6 7 8 9 10

BOOK DESIGN BERNARD SCHLEIFER

To Irene,
who enriches my life
366 days of each year

INTRODUCTION

How to Use This Book

You and I are about to become partners in the writing of this book. I have provided a perennial almanac in which you will find curious, captivating, or humorous information about every day of the year. You can add the important events of your life, along with those of friends and family, including annual dates you wish to remember, so it becomes a personal and useful record.

Every Day a Celebration

The almanac provides you with a celebration for every day of the year. Approaching each new day as an event you can honor, or at least observe, can add a touch of zest to your daily routine. At a practical level, knowing that each day is special provides you with an effective icebreaker or opener for beginning a conversation or a meeting.

Every Day a Smile

Each day, the almanac provides a variety of adages, epigrams, one-liners, or historical information that may help you smile as you face your daily responsibilities, tribulations, and accomplishments.

Every Day a Thought

A satirical and sometimes cynical theory, law, principle, or rule appears at the bottom of each page to help focus our thoughts on our foibles and frailties. These generalizations about life may not always contain the whole truth but have enough validity to justify our reflection and consideration.

Personal Chronicle

A chronicle is defined as a chronological record of historical events. If you record events related to your life, in the blank spaces provided on each page, you will be creating your own personal chronicle. Begin by writing the events you wish to remember on the appropriately dated pages. This will be not only a valuable, permanent record of family birthdays, anniversaries, and so forth, but also a reminder of other entertaining and important events that occurred on these personally special days. Continue to make entries as new special happenings occur. Family reunions, important meetings, major purchases, job changes, mortgage burnings, and all the things that make changes in your life or that you feel are significant, are suitable entries. Your personal chronicle can then become a treasured possession, a source of nostalgia and enjoyment, and a valued family record.

—LAURENCE J. PETER

NOTE: Each day in this almanac is a special event with its own title. Many of the days are traditional celebrations, some are official holidays or observances, and some are named by the author for an event that happened on that date. The information contained herein has been gathered over the years from a wide variety of sources, including newspapers, encyclopedias, chronologies, old almanacs, calendars, history books, and other reference works. Celebrating special days has been a tradition throughout human history. I have labelled and described each day as an event to celebrate but have left the type of observance up to the reader. For those who would like more information about days that have organized observances, including the names and addresses of sponsors of special events, the most useful reference is Chases' Calendar of Annual Events, published by Apple Tree Press, Inc., Box 1012, Flint, Michigan 48501.

JANUARY 1, the first day of the Gregorian calendar year, is a public holiday in most countries. It has been the beginning of the year in English-speaking countries since the British Calendar Act of 1751. The month is named in honor of Janus, the god that presides over doors and therefore has jurisdiction over the opening of the year. It is traditionally a time for new beginnings and making resolutions for the coming year. It also is a time for recovering from New Year's Eve festivities. These activities are somewhat incompatible as resolution-making should be based on clear thinking.

You're only young once, but you can be childish all your life.

There is no shortcut to longevity.

How uninteresting would be the sounds of nature if we only heard from the Top Ten birds.

On January 1, 1764, Wolfgang Amadeus Mozart, then eight years of age, played for the Royal Family at Versailles, after which he was allowed to stand behind the queen at dinner.

Peter's New Year's Day Principle: The fizz of a glass of Bromo Seltzer can sound as loud as a room full of rowdies the night before.

FIRST UNITED STATES FLAG DAY

ON THIS DAY IN 1776, George Washington, the commander-in-chief of the Continental Army, designed a flag that was raised at his headquarters in Cambridge, Massachusetts. It consisted of the Union Jack—the British flag—in the corner now occupied by stars, on a background of thirteen red and white stripes representing the thirteen colonies.

The second day of a New Year's resolution is easier than the first, if by then you've broken it.

Two's company. Three's a trend.

Give a child enough rope and he'll trip you up.

There will always be adult education—as long as parents continue to help children with their homework.

The Dime Book of Practical Etiquette was published on January 2, 1859, by Erastus F. Beadle.

Peter's Political Principle: No candidate tells the people that he wants power over them, so he tells them that he wants to help them.

SAINT GENEVIEVE'S FEAST DAY

THIS IS THE FEAST DAY of St. Genevieve, patron saint of Paris. Her prayers are said to have averted Attila the Hun's attack on the city in A.D. 451. Whether her prayers were responsible or not, we can all admire her good intentions.

Peter Principle I: In a hierarchy individuals tend to rise to their level of incompetence.

Peter Principle II: The cream rises until it sours.

Peter Principle III: For every job that exists in the world, there is someone, somewhere, who can't do it. Given enough promotions, that incompetent will get the job.

Peter Principle IV: A journey of 1,000 miles ends with but a single step.

Peter Principle V: All useful work is accomplished by individuals who have not yet reached their level of incompetence.

Peter's Reflection on the Peter Principle: A principle is not responsible for the people who believe in it.

ON JANUARY 4, 1885, Mary Gartside of Davenport, Iowa, became the first American to have her appendix removed.

I heard of a young man who had to give up the study of surgery—couldn't stand the sight of money.

I tried to tell my son the facts of life, but I kept getting into a debate.

It is hard to be independent all by yourself.

A drowning man will clutch at a strawberry blonde.

On this day in 1899, a chambermaid in a Canary Islands hotel saw Camille Saint-Saëns writing a musical score. Thinking him a spy writing in code, she reported him to the police.

Peter's Employment Principle: Don't knock the rich—when did a poor person ever give you a job?

EIGHT-HOUR, FIVE-DOLLAR DAY

ON JANUARY 5, 1914, James Cousens, general manager of the Ford Motor Company, announced the doubling of the wage scale, inaugurating the five-dollar-a-day minimum wage and the reduction of the workday from nine to eight hours. The Ford management claimed this "the greatest revolution in the matter of rewards for its workers ever known in the industrial world."

If you can't understand something as constant as $E = MC^2$, how can you ever understand something as complex and variable as another human being?

Anything that's only moderately overpriced is a bargain.

You're really an optimist if you watch the six o'clock, seven o'clock, and ten o'clock news, hoping it will get better.

On this day in 1778 a grand scheme to destroy the British fleet, in the Delaware River near Philadelphia, turned out to be a complete flop. The first American contact mines were set afloat by David Bushnell, but none of them worked, so the British Navy was undisturbed.

Peter's Theory of Child Development: Children grow up quickly these days—many teenagers are already confused, discouraged, and broke.

TWELFTH DAY   *January 6*

THE FEAST OF EPIPHANY was celebrated in most European countries on the twelfth day after Christmas. This is one of the oldest Christian feasts and celebrates the visit of the Magi, the first Gentile recognition of Christ. Epiphany or Twelfth Day is observed in many Christian Churches today.

If violence on television causes violence in the streets, why doesn't singing on television cause singing in the streets?

If at first you don't succeed, try, try again—to understand the directions.

You're in trouble if you are looking for a custom fit in this off-the-rack world.

On January 6, 1640, the Virginia General Assembly ordered half the tobacco crop burned because a surplus had reduced prices, indicating that government interference with free enterprise is a longstanding tradition.

Peter's Timing Principle: Today is the day of decision, unless you're on the other side of the international date line where it was yesterday.

THE PANAMA CANAL was successfully navigated for the first time on January 7, 1914. The canal, also called the Big Ditch, was started under the administration of President Teddy Roosevelt. This day marks the beginning of a significant improvement in American maritime transportation and a significant deterioration of relations with the Republic of Panama. The canal is a triumph of American engineering and a Panamanian political triumph as they now have the Big Ditch.

We're all brothers under the skin, but some brothers get under your skin more than others.

Political success is the ability, when the inevitable occurs, to get credit for it.

All is fair in love and the war that follows.

On January 7, 1896, Fannie Farmer published her first cookbook. Since then her cookbooks have been continuous best sellers.

Peter's Balanced-Budget Principle: They said it couldn't be done. I'll go along with that.

JACKSON DAY   *January 8*

JANUARY 8, 1815, is also known as Old Hickory Day and Battle of New Orleans Day, because that was when United States troops led by General Andrew Jackson inflicted over 2,000 casualties, bringing about a crushing defeat of the British forces. Unfortunately this last battle of the War of 1812 was fought two weeks after the war was over. The signing of the Treaty of Ghent on December 24, 1814, had officially ended the hostilities, but the message had not been received by either army. Andrew Jackson became a great American hero for this postwar military victory.

You should never ever be absolute in anything you say.

A Rolling Stone gathers screaming teenagers.

An optimist is someone who thinks the E on the gas gauge stands for Enough.

On January 8, 1918, President Woodrow Wilson, in his Fourteen-Points speech to a joint session of Congress, outlined the peace aims of the U.S. in World War I.

Peter's Mental-Health Principle: The only positive thing about a nervous breakdown is that it shows that you really care.

FIRST BALLOON FLIGHT DAY   *January 9*

ON JANUARY 9, 1793, Jean Pierre Blanchard soared above the courtyard of the Germantown Prison in the first successful balloon flight in the United States. The takeoff was witnessed by a large, excited crowd, including President Washington, Thomas Jefferson, John Adams, Henry Clay, and Paul Revere. Blanchard sailed over Philadelphia and landed about 46 minutes later at Woodbury, New Jersey, completing a 15-mile flight.

It's love that makes the world.

If we learn by our mistakes, we should have the best government on earth.

Better to have loved and lost than never to have lost at all.

On January 9, 1873, Reverend Henry Ward Beecher, the most popular preacher of his time, was charged with adultery in connection with a suit by Theodore Tilton alleging alienation of his wife's affections. Beecher escaped on a legal technicality and drew larger crowds than ever, particularly when he preached on sin.

Peter's Family Principle: I love my children, but I can't stand the younger generation.

ON JANUARY 10, 1931, at a premier of "Three Places in New England," composer Charles Ives, in response to boos and hisses, addressed the audience as "sissy-eared," and told them to "stand up and use your ears like a man."

He who fights and runs away may live to take flight another day.

We know that life is a gamble, but we continue to build a system on each random success.

A meeting of minds is preferable to bumping of heads.

On January 10, 1928, Leon Trotsky, heir apparent to Lenin, was exiled to Kazakhstan and later banished from Russia. Subsequently he was murdered in 1940 in a suburb of Mexico City.

Peter's Truth Principle: Politicians try to tell us what they think we want to hear; prophets try to tell us what is right.

ON JANUARY 11, 1759, the first life-insurance company in America was founded. It was named the Corporation for Relief of Poor and Distressed Widows and Children of Presbyterian Ministers.

He laughs best whose laugh lasts.

One hand washes the other and together they lose the soap.

If you think there are two sides to the argument, you're not in it.

On January 11, 1925, Walter Damrosch conducted Aaron Copeland's Symphony for Organ and Orchestra and announced to the audience that a man who at 23 can compose this music "will in five years be ready to commit murder."

Peter's TV Principle: They tell us, "The public gets what it wants," when in truth it gets what it gets.

ON JANUARY 12, 1896, Dr. H. L. Smith, a professor of astronomy at Davidson College, made the first X-ray photograph in the United States and became the first doctor to have real inside information.

"Prevention is better than being cured," said the pig as he made his escape.

You owe it to yourself to become a success. After that you owe it to the IRS.

Blessed are the pure in heart for they shall inhibit the earth.

On January 12, 1979, President Carter fired Bella Abzug as cochairperson of the National Advisory Committee on Women.

Peter's Energy Principle: Air-flight wastes fuel—my suitcase has traveled 11,000 miles farther than I have.

NATIONAL PRINTING INK DAY

THE NATIONAL ASSOCIATION of Printing Ink Manufacturers has identified this day as the one on which to honor the contributions that printing ink makes to the graphic arts and the communication industries and to the dissemination of knowledge, culture, education, and entertainment. We can all enthusiastically endorse these sentiments, except when it comes off our newspapers and blackens our hands or new white shirts.

Hollywood movies could be improved greatly if they shot less film and more producers.

Too many people are digging up their roots when they should be cultivating their sprouts.

Children have an important role to play in the survival-of-the-fittest scheme of things. The world would have an oversupply of antique furniture without them.

January 13, 1808, is the birth date of the only Chief Justice to be named after a fish, Lincoln's Secretary of the Treasury, Salmon P. Chase.

Peter's Saving Principle: A fool and his money are soon parted—just like the rest of us.

ON JANUARY 14, 1914, Henry Ford started the assembly line that reduced the time of putting together a car from 12½ hours to 93 minutes. This contributed to lowered automobile prices, traffic jams, smog, energy shortages, and Arab financial dominance of petroleum prices.

Your automobile repair bills may be an example of a lemon putting the squeeze on you.

The early worm is for the birds.

I knew he was stoned when he scratched himself and missed.

On January 14, 1979, the Census Bureau said that 95 percent of all Americans are married or will get married. It also said that the divorce rate had doubled since 1960, but that most divorcees ultimately remarry.

Peter's Sexual Principle: The devil finds work for idle glands.

MARTIN LUTHER KING, JR.'S BIRTHDAY   *January 15*

THE PREEMINENT BLACK civil-rights leader, Martin Luther King, Jr., was born on January 15, 1929, in Atlanta, Georgia. A Christian minister, he followed the example of Gandhi in recommending passive resistance as a means of social protest. He won the Nobel Peace Prize in 1964 and was assassinated in 1968.

America has not turned out to be a melting pot. It is more like granola—full of nuts, fruits, and flakes.

I have this pain that comes every 20 minutes and lasts for an hour.

Common sense could save many marriages. If we used it there wouldn't be so many.

This is also Molière Day. On January 15, 1622, Jean Baptiste Poquelin took the stage name Molière. He became the most celebrated French author and dramatist. In 1673, while acting in his last play, *La Malade Imaginaire*, a story about hypochondria, he took ill and died within a few hours.

Peter's Sportsmanship Principle: It is easy to spot the winners—they're the ones not complaining about the rules.

AMERICAN AUTONOMY DAY   *January 16*

ON JANUARY 16, 1778, France initiated recognition of the autonomy of the United States, thus contributing to America's winning the Revolutionary War and achieving independence.

Television enables people with nothing to do to watch people who can do nothing.

Bankruptcy is never having to say you're sorry.

January 16 is also National Nothing Day.

When I die I wish my mortal remains to be cremated and the ashes sent to the Internal Revenue Service with a note saying, "Now you have it all."

On this day in 1920, Prohibition went into effect.

Peter's Miracle Principle: Two tiny demichromosomed pre-protozoan flecks of amino acids unite and develop into the awesome complexity of a human being.

BENJAMIN FRANKLIN'S BIRTHDAY

THE OLDEST SIGNER of both the Declaration of Independence and the Constitution of the United States, Benjamin Franklin, elder statesman of the American revolution, was born in Boston on January 17, 1706. He achieved fame in 21 lines of endeavor. He was a philosopher, statesman, man of letters, journalist, author, essayist, printer, publisher, economist, scientist, linguist, inventor, politician, capitalist, engineer, educator, diplomat, abolitionist, humanitarian, historian, and mathematician. He attended school for only two years.

Death is nature's way of preventing you from inhaling smog.

Maybe the meek shall inherit the earth, but how long will they be able to keep it?

All men are created equal but some aren't equal to much.

On January 17, 1779, Captain James Cook named the Sandwich Islands after Lord Sandwich, head of the British Admiralty. The Sandwich Islands are now called the Hawaiian Islands.

Peter's Specialization Principle: We live in the age of specialization where nine out of ten specialists are so specialized that they have to recommend other specialists.

ON JANUARY 18, 1944, the first concert of jazz music at the Metropolitan Opera House was performed in this stately temple of classical music in New York City. Appearing on the program, among others, were Louis Armstrong, Big Sid Catlett, Lionel Hampton, Roy Eldridge, Jack Teagarden, Benny Goodman, and Artie Shaw.

Old age and treachery can always defeat youth and skill.

If killing people is crude, then "sophisticated weapons" is a contradiction in terms.

It is silly to call money "dough" when it doesn't stick to your fingers.

The problem of doing nothing is that you don't know when quitting time is.

On January 18, 1943, during World War II, bakers in America were ordered to quit selling sliced bread for the duration. Although this imposed a sacrifice on housewives and others throughout the United States, how it helped the war effort was never explained or understood.

Peter's Patriotic Principle: We should be united by loved things held in common rather than by fear of foreign ideologies.

A SYSTEM FOR MAKING color motion pictures, invented by Dr. Herbert Kalmus, was used in a film, *The Gulf Between*, and copyrighted January 19, 1918.

I watched a long love scene at the movies and then I realized I was facing the wrong way.

Jack left his position with the rock group because the noise was too much. He went back to his old job at the boiler factory.

On January 19, 1903, the first regular transatlantic radio broadcast was sent between Cape Cod, Massachusetts, and Cornwall, England.

Always remember that true beauty comes from within—from within bottles, jars, compacts, and tubes.

On January 19, 1949, Congress raised the salary of the President of the United States from $75,000 to $100,000. Although the President has received several raises since, the working conditions have not improved.

Peter's Advice Principle: We would all be more willing to accept good advice if it didn't always interfere with our plans.

FIRST PARLIAMENT DAY   *January 20*

ON JANUARY 20, 1265, in the reign of King Henry III, the Earl of Leicester, Simon de Montfort, called the first English Parliament to meet at the hall at Westminster. Until this time, only councils of the lords or large landholders had been held. This was the first at which commoners were represented, there being two knights from each county and two commoners from each borough. This day marks a major breakthrough in our progress toward a democratic form of government.

I seldom buy my wife anything. I'm a man of rare gifts.

Old accountants never die, they just don't count anymore.

Insomnia is not worth losing sleep over.

Every fourth year, this is also Presidential Inauguration Day. The Twentieth Amendment to the Constitution requires that the President and Vice President end their term of office at noon on this day and that their successors' terms begin at that time.

Peter's Safety Principle: There were few accidents in the horse and buggy days because drivers didn't rely completely on their own intelligence.

BETTER WORKING CONDITIONS DAY

January 21

ON JANUARY 21, 1919, New York garment workers, 35,000 strong, went on strike for a 44-hour week. The success of this strike was pivotal in the improvement of industrial working conditions.

Food is a consuming passion.

Nothing curbs a child's appetite like making him sit still at the dinner table.

A really ill child is one that gets sick on Saturday morning.

A child with big ideas is one who is working on increasing his allowance.

On January 21, 1979, men in Iowa's North County resigned themselves to having their hair cut in the local beauty shops because the last barbershop in the area closed.

Peter's Social Principle: Don't try to keep up with the Joneses until you know where they're going.

DANCE OF THE SEVEN VEILS DAY

ON JANUARY 22, 1907, the premiere of the Richard Strauss opera *Salome*, with its Dance of the Seven Veils, inspired vaudeville performers everywhere to do their own version of the "naughty" dance. The directors of the Metropolitan Opera Company were so shocked by the opera, and by this turn of events, that they prohibited further performances by the Met.

The problem when you hit middle age is the way it hits back.

On January 22, 1575, Queen Elizabeth granted William Byrd and Thomas Tallis a monopoly for printing and selling music paper.

You're in jeopardy if you live in a high-crime area—like the USA.

On January 22, 1789, the first American novel, *The Power of Sympathy*, was published. It was a story of lust, seduction, incest, and suicide that set the pattern for American novelists.

Peter's Laughter Principle: A sense of humor is what makes you laugh at things that would annoy you if they happened to you.

NATIONAL HANDWRITING DAY

THIS DAY IS observed to encourage more legible handwriting. It provides Americans with a demonstrable way of honoring their pioneer patriot and statesman John Hancock, who was born on this day in 1737 in Braintree, Massachusetts. He was the first signer of the Declaration of Independence, causing his name to become synonymous with the word *signature*.

Since inflation I've been living in the lapse of luxury.

He was so generous with his girl friend he had to marry her for her money.

Spending money is my wife's only extravagance.

On January 23, 1843, the composer Anton Bruckner, working as assistant schoolmaster in Winhaag, was sent to the miserable hamlet of Kromstorf for refusing to shovel dung.

Peter's People Types:
1. People who make things happen.
2. People who watch things happen.
3. People who don't know what happened.

On January 24, 1848, gold was discovered on the property of John A. Sutter in California. This led to the Gold Rush and the forty-niners.

Good fences make good neighbors—and good neighbors make good fences.

On January 24, 1899, Humphrey O'Sullivan of Lowell, Massachusetts, patented the rubber heel.

When I made fun of the scantiness of her bikini, she just laughed it off.

On this day in 1935 the first beer in cans was sold.

Peter's Audubon Principle: The only way to positively identify a bird is to be with a group of people who don't know much either.

ROBERT BURNS, BELOVED SCOTTISH POET, was born at Ayrshire, Scotland, January 25, 1759. Burns Day is widely celebrated, especially in Scotland and England and by Burns Clubs and Scottish societies worldwide. The traditional Burns Dinner is centered around the haggis, which consists of a mixture of minced heart, lungs, and liver of sheep or calf with suet, oatmeal, and onions sewn in the stomach of the animal and then boiled for hours. The event features speeches and toasts to the memory of Robert Burns and outpourings of patriotism and sentiment for "Dear Old Scotland."

"Oh wad some power the giftie gie us
To see oursels as others see us!"—we'd all be in depression.

If you want a thing well done—cook it yourself.

January 25 is also Saint Paul's Day, and according to an old belief, if the sun shines today it means a good year.

Peter's Prescription: If at first you do succeed, try not to look too astonished.

On JANUARY 26, 1784, in a letter to his daughter, Sarah Bache, Benjamin Franklin disapproved of the eagle as a symbol of the United States when he stated, "I wish the Bald Eagle had not been chosen as the Representative of our Country; he is a Bird of bad moral Character; like those among Men who live by Sharping and Robbing, he is generally poor, and often very lousy. The Turkey is a much more respectable Bird, and withal a true original Native of America."

By the time I'm put out to pasture, Social Security will be out of grass.

You had better learn from the mistakes of others—you don't have enough time to make them all yourself.

Middle age is feeling bad in the morning after no fun the night before.

On January 26, 1838, Tennessee became the first state to enact a prohibition law "to repeal all laws licensing tippling houses." The effect of the law was to increase illegal drinking and improve the financial status of bootleggers and moonshiners.

———

Peter's Jealousy Principle: Sour grapes can upset your apple cart.

ON JANUARY 27, 1973, peace accords were signed in Paris by North and South Vietnam, the United States, and the National Liberation Front. This ended the United States combat role in an undeclared war which had involved Americans since the defeated French had left under terms of the Geneva Accords of 1954. This was the longest war in United States history.

It's easy to get children to tread the straight and narrow path. Just live in a corner house and try to grow a lawn.

The cause of a child's developing class hatred is forcing him to repeat a year in one.

A child who is two jumps ahead of his class is the one who can read the clock.

On this day in 1967, the *Apollo I* spacecraft caught fire.

Peter's Genius Principle: A real genius is someone who can aim at something nobody else sees, and hit it.

IN 1754, HORACE WALPOLE, the English writer, read a fairy tale called *The Travels and Adventures of Three Princes of Serendip*. He was delighted with the three heroes from Serendip (the early name for Ceylon, now called Sri Lanka) and their many chance discoveries. Walpole was so impressed with the princes' capacity for making accidental discoveries that in a letter written on January 28, 1754, he created the word *serendipity* to describe this ability. This is one of the rare words whose date of origin can be documented, as most words evolve over a period of years.

Cleanliness is not next to godliness. I looked it up in the dictionary and godlike is next to godliness.

Our local postmaster is mad at me just because I turned in the name of our mailman to the Missing Persons Bureau.

There are three types of politicians: the dedicated, the honest, and the majority.

On this day in 1807, London's Pall Mall became the first street in the world to be illuminated with gaslight.

Peter's Perception Principle: If your view is really great, it may be because you can't see the house you're looking from.

ON THIS DAY in 1880 William Claude Dukenfield (W. C. Fields) was born in Philadelphia to "poor but dishonest parents." He became a vaudeville juggler, a comedian, and a movie star. As a writer and performer of comedy, he was in a class by himself. He thought funny. He looked funny. He walked funny. He moved and juggled funny. He sounded funny. His performances were a confluence of all the elements of his comic character. Many of his irreverent lines have become comedy classics.

"Anything worth having is worth cheating for."
"Thou shalt not commit adultery . . . unless in the mood."
"A man who doesn't drink isn't a fit companion for man or beast."
"A wonderful drink, wine . . . did you ever hear of an Italian grape crusher with athlete's foot?"
"I am very humble—and proud of it."

The post office issued a W. C. Fields stamp on his birthday . . . which is ironic when you consider he had such a good delivery.

On January 29, 1936, the first five players were elected to the Baseball Hall of Fame: Ty Cobb, Babe Ruth, Honus Wagner, Christy Mathewson, and Walter Johnson.

Peter's Age Prescription: When wine, women, and song become too much, stop singing.

SAINT CHARLES'S DAY   *January 30*

ANNUALLY ON THIS DAY, the Society of Saint Charles the Martyr conducts a memorial service at the site of the scaffold at the Royal United Services Museum in London. During the civil strife in England between forces loyal to King Charles and those loyal to Parliament, the king was beheaded on a scaffold in front of the Banqueting House at Whitehall, January 30, 1649. After his execution the state of Virginia declared its allegiance to his family, the House of Stuart, resulting in 330 loyalists taking refuge in Virginia that year.

The person who boasts about getting up at dawn to see the sun rise could hardly have picked a better time.

There are more things in life than money. There are also credit cards and overdrafts.

On January 30, 1933, Adolf Hitler became chancellor of Germany, and the radio program *The Lone Ranger* first went on the air. On this day in 1882 Franklin Delano Roosevelt was born, in 1917 the first United States jazz record was cut, in 1923 Carol Channing was born, and in 1948 Mahatma Gandhi was assassinated.

Peter's Longevity Principle: To live longer all you have to do is stop doing the things that make you want to live longer.

THE ELECTIVE FRANCHISE ACT of January 30, 1867, provided that there should be no denial of elective franchise to any United States citizen on account of race, color, or previous condition of servitude. Just because implementation of this act was delayed in some states should not be a reason for failing to honor it as a landmark decision.

I don't mind surprises—provided I'm prepared for them.

I told my son he would have to learn to shift for himself. He said, "Great, you're buying me a sports car."

Television was invented by an impatient man who wanted pictures to look at while waiting for something good on the radio.

On January 31, 1797, Franz Schubert was born in Himmelpfortgrund near Vienna.

Peter's Status Quo Theory: When conditions of any organization are changed, the whole organization will shift in an attempt to restore the original condition.

February

NATIONAL FREEDOM DAY   *February 1*

IN THE UNITED STATES this day is celebrated to mark the 1865 signing of the Thirteenth Amendment to the American Constitution abolishing slavery. In 1949, a Presidential Proclamation established National Freedom Day as an annual event in perpetuity.

Programs on TV are sandwiched between the commercials as packing to protect them—like Styrofoam around a small appliance.

Give a metric-system advocate an inch and he'll take 1.6 kilometers.

What we really need most is to realize how little we really need.

On February 1, 1892, the list of 400 guests for Mrs. William B. Astor's society ball in New York City made "the 400" synonymous with high society.

Peter's Financial Principle I: Starting from scratch is easy; starting without it is tough.

EACH YEAR ON FEBRUARY 2, in Punxsutawney, Pennsylvania, people gather to wait for a groundhog to emerge and see his shadow, which means winter is not yet over, or not see it, which means spring is on its way. Naturalists know that no groundhog in its right mind leaves its snug hibernation to appear on Groundhog Day. Celebrate, today, either nature's wisdom or human gullibility.

We need political conventions to decide who's going to be the life of the party.

I knew a fellow who was so unlucky he got into accidents that started out happening to someone else.

You'll find that life is easy once you've learned to accept the impossible, do without the essential, and bear the intolerable.

On February 2, 1893, a cameraman at Thomas Edison's moving-picture studio in West Orange, New Jersey, took the first close-up in motion-picture history. It was of comedian Fred Ott sneezing.

Peter's Financial Principle II: After a raise in salary you will have less money at the end of the month than you had before.

WHAT IS NOW the state of Illinois was originally included in the vast area of the Northwest Territory. On February 3, 1809, an act was approved setting up the territory of Illinois. A constitution was framed and Illinois became a state in 1818.

If at first you don't succeed, try, try, again—when nobody's watching.

It's hard to convince a sunburn victim that the sun is 93 million miles away.

Cheer up—things can only get better, or worse, or stay the same.

On February 3, 1979, Bonnie Sue Davenport, formerly Ormus Davenport, III, became the first transsexual on the Washington, D.C., police force.

Peter's Financial Principle III: Every time history repeats itself the prices go up.

MARK HOPKINS DAY   *February 4*

ONE OF THE MOST distinguished educators of his generation, Mark Hopkins was born in Stockbridge, Massachusetts, on February 4, 1802. He was a competent scholar, but it was as a teacher that he achieved his great fame. He was able to arouse such interest, curiosity, and enthusiasm that President James A. Garfield said that all that was needed for a superior education was Mark Hopkins sitting on one end of a log and a student on the other.

You can be too helpful—like throwing a drowning man both ends of the rope.

If you think it's hard to move mountains, you've never had to mark sixth-grade geography papers.

Now that I'm retired, I'm still kicking but not raising much dust.

On February 4, 1789, the Electoral College named George Washington the President of the United States.

Peter's Financial Principle IV: The man who writes the advertisements for the bank is not the guy who makes the loans.

THIS DAY COMMEMORATES the birth of America's first weatherman, John Jeffries, on February 5, 1744. Jeffries, a Boston physician, kept detailed records of the weather conditions from 1774 to 1816, with an interruption from 1776 to 1790 when, as a Loyalist, he was obliged to leave Boston with the British Army. He returned to Boston after establishing a new career in England as a balloonist—crossing the English Channel January 7, 1785, and four days later dining in Paris with Benjamin Franklin, American ambassador to France and a fellow student of weather.

It pays to be courteous. Yesterday I gave my place in the checkout line to a man with only two items—a note and a gun.

Before credit cards, I knew exactly how much I was broke.

Life is like a taxi ride—the meter keeps on ticking whether you're getting anywhere or not.

Mexico Constitution Day commemorates two events: the promulgation of the liberal Constitution of 1857, and the February 5, 1917, adoption of the present Constitution.

Peter's Financial Principle V: An economist can take something you already know and make it confusing.

LAME DUCK
AMENDMENT DAY

February 6

THE TWENTIETH AMENDMENT to the Constitution of the United States was proclaimed in effect on February 6, 1933. It specified that the President's and Vice President's terms of office should begin on January 20, senators' and representatives' on January 3 instead of March 4, and that Congress should convene on January 3 instead of the first Monday in December. This amendment eliminated the short December session of Congress, which had included members who had been defeated in November, popularly called "lame ducks."

You can get just as drunk on water as you can on dry land.

The purpose of celebrating February 6 as Midwinter Day is to observe that winter is half over and to create euphoria by stating the fact, or by fiat.

If you come out of the laundry with an even number of socks, you have somebody else's laundry.

On February 6, 1843, *The Virginia Minstrels*, the first minstrel show in America, was opened in the Bowery Amphitheatre in New York, by Dan Emmett.

Peter Financial Principle VI: If your outgo exceeds your income, your upkeep is your downfall.

ON FEBRUARY 7, 1778, Daniel Boone and about 30 other men engaged in making salt at Blue Licks, Kentucky, were captured by Indians and all except Daniel Boone were delivered to the English commander in York. Boone was taken to Chilicote where he made a daring escape and walked 160 miles through the forest to freedom.

The best time to buy a used car is when it's new.

The walls in this apartment are so thin that when I asked my wife a question, I got four different answers.

Until 1967 I never had an accident; that was the year I bought a car.

February 7, 1882, was the day of the last bareknuckle world's heavyweight boxing championship contest. John L. Sullivan knocked out Paddy Ryan in the ninth round in Mississippi City.

Peter's Financial Principle VII: Two can live as cheaply as one—for about half as long.

TODAY OBSERVES THE ANNIVERSARY of the chartering of the Boy Scouts of America on February 8, 1910. The organization of boys into a society of scouts was originated by an Englishman, Sir Robert S. S. Baden-Powell, and today includes millions of members throughout the world.

A good cure for a hangover is to drink black coffee the night before instead of the morning after.

Isabella Chambers, a 24-year-old New Yorker became the first American woman to purchase life insurance when she took out a $2,000 policy on February 8, 1843.

During the garbage strike, for the first time there was more trash in the streets than on TV.

The original version of the movie *Getting Gertie's Garter* opened on February 8, 1927.

Peter's Financial Principle VIII: There is no such thing as a cheap politician.

IN ALEXANDRIA, on February 9, 249, during the persecution of Christians, Saint Apollonia was seized, and all her teeth were beaten out with a stone. She was then threatened with being cast into the fire if she did not utter certain impious words. This she declined to do and of her own accord leaped into the fire. Because of the nature of her persecution and her self-sacrifice, Apollonia became the patron saint of persons afflicted with toothache and of the dentists who treat them.

The mechanic advised me to keep the oil and change the car.

I attribute my age to being born a long time ago.

Although I only use two fingers, I can still type faster than I think.

On February 9, 1825, because the Electoral College failed to give any candidate a majority, the House of Representatives elected John Quincy Adams sixth President of the United States. Adams was the son of John Adams, second U.S. President.

Peter's Financial Principle IX: Each slight tax increase costs you $800 and each substantial tax cut saves you 45 cents.

SAINT SCHOLASTICA'S DAY *February 10*

SAINT SCHOLASTICA, a virgin martyr and patron saint of scholars, died on February 10, 543. On Saint Scholastica's Day in 1354 a violent conflict occurred between the students of the University of Oxford and the townspeople. The citizens of the town called for the aid of the country folk from nearby, and together they overpowered the scholars, killing and wounding several of their number. As a consequence, the citizens were denied certain church consolations and their privileges were restricted. By way of a penance forever it was decreed that on each Saint Scholastica's Day the mayor and 62 citizens attend St. Mary's Church and that each man make an offering of one penny.

In the past we had to solve the problems we found, and today we have to solve the problems we create.

Old salesmen never die—they just go out of commission.

On February 10, 1965, Hubert H. Humphrey said, "The impersonal hand of government can never replace the helping hand of a neighbor."

Peter's Financial Principle X: Money is a fringe benefit of success.

ON FEBRUARY 11, 1979, Shirley Ravenscroft, 53, became the first grandmother to sail the Atlantic alone when she landed in Barbados after a 37-day voyage in a 26-foot sailboat.

There were so many celebrities there that I was the only one I hadn't heard of before.

On February 11, 1979, Barbara S. Askins received the Inventor of the Year award for designing an autoradiographic-image-enhancement process that reduced X-ray exposure.

You know you're an old-timer if you recall when what you got for nothing didn't cost you so much.

On February 11, 1968, the present Madison Square Garden, the third to be so named, was opened in New York.

Peter's Financial Principle XI: Put a little money away each month and at the end of the year you will be surprised how little you have.

EMANCIPATION OF JAZZ DAY *February 12*

ON FEBRUARY 12, 1924, a landmark concert took place in New York's Aeolian Hall when Paul Whiteman conducted a program of "symphonic jazz" in which the highlight was the first public performance of Rhapsody in Blue with George Gershwin at the piano. The cheering audience included John Philip Sousa, Walter Damrosch, Leopold Godowsky, Jascha Heifetz, Fritz Kreisler, Sergei Rachmaninoff, Leopold Stokowski, Mischa Elman, and Igor Stravinsky. Because it was Lincoln's birthday, the concert was described as The Emancipation Proclamation of Jazz.

A rare book is one that's returned after you loan it.

On February 12, 1974, the first Susan B. Anthony silver dollar was struck at the U.S. Mint in Philadelphia. The coin looked so much like a quarter that this intended tribute was underwhelming.

I can remember when being an eccentric was an eccentricity.

Today is the birthday of Abraham Lincoln, sixteenth President of the United States. Of the occasion he said, "I was born February 12, 1809, in the then Hardin County, Kentucky, at a point within the new county of Larue, a mile or a mile and a half from where Hodgen's mill now is."

Peter's Financial Principle XII: Money is the root of all evil—and we all need roots.

EXORBITANT PRICE DAY   *February 13*

ON FEBRUARY 13, 1914, the movie *Joseph in the Land of Egypt* opened with a new high in admission, 50 cents. Moviegoers' complaints about the exorbitantly high price made the headlines.

Although I love traveling, I wasn't even slightly interested in his ego trip.

On February 13, 1635, the Boston Latin School, the oldest public school in America, was established in Boston, Massachusetts.

He only drinks for medicinal purposes—can't leave being well enough alone.

On February 13, 1747, the first magazine to be published in America, *The American Magazine*, was issued by Andrew Bradford in Philadelphia.

Peter's Accuracy Principle: Nothing can be totaled correctly after 4:37 P.M. on Friday.

THERE ARE A VARIETY of theories regarding the origin of this day upon which lovers send tokens of affection to each other. One of the more attractive is based on the belief, held throughout Europe in the Middle Ages, that birds began to mate on February 14. The name of the day is derived from three Saint Valentines, each of whom was associated with February 14.

I hate to have nothing to do because it provides no opportunities to stop and rest.

On February 14, 1894, Benny Kubelsky, later to become famous as the American comedian Jack Benny, was born in Waukegan, Illinois.

It's easy to understand modern art—if it hangs on the wall, it's a painting; if you can walk around it, it's a sculpture.

Bela Lugosi's original Dracula movie was released February 14, 1931. Dracula's drinking problem became the basis of more than 100 vampire films to follow.

Peter's Forecasting Rule: When working toward a solution, it always helps if you know the answer beforehand.

THE ANNIVERSARY of the birth of woman suffrage leader Susan B. Anthony, February 15, 1820, is observed annually as Susan B. Anthony Day. Memorial tributes to her leadership vary from eulogies in Congress to special school programs honoring the contributions of women. Toward the end of her life Susan B. Anthony said, "I have been striving for over sixty years for a little bit of justice . . . and yet I must die without obtaining it."

A responsible citizen is one who votes my way.

On February 15, 1965, with a 21-gun salute on Parliament Hill in Ottawa, Canada unfurled its new red and white national Maple Leaf Flag.

We must be making progress—every year it takes less time to fly across the ocean and longer to drive to work.

On February 15, 1842, the first postage stamps in the United States with adhesive on the back were introduced by a private mail service in New York.

Peter's First-Amendment Principle: What this country needs is more free speech worth listening to.

TELEVISION NEWS DAY   *February 16*

On February 16, 1948, the first daily television news was broadcast on NBC.

Inflation is when it takes all you've got to keep up with the losers.

On February 16, 1607, the neighborhood children serenaded Archdeacon John Spratt of St. David's Church in London:

> Jack Sprat could eat no fat,
> His wife could eat no lean,
> And so betwixt them both, you see
> They licked the platter clean.

He was a dainty eater and she had a huge appetite so people tried to ask him to dinner without inviting her.

Classified ad: George. Get in touch as soon as possible. Bring three rings—engagement, wedding, and teething. Have news. Doris.

On February 16, 1868, members of "The Jolly Gorks," a social and benevolent society, organized themselves into a new organization called the Benevolent and Protective Order of Elks. Their purpose was to practice charity, justice, brotherly love, and faithfulness.

Peter's Bilateral Law: The left hand of government doesn't know what the right hand is doing—and doesn't know what the left is doing either.

PTA FOUNDER'S DAY

THE PTA WAS FOUNDED in the United States on February 17, 1897, as the National Congress of Mothers and was later expanded to include fathers, teachers, and other citizens. Today the official name of the organization commonly known as the PTA is the National Congress of Parents and Teachers. The purpose of this special day is to honor Alice McLellan Birney and Phoebe Apperson Hearst, founders of the National PTA, and Selena Sloan Butler, founder of the National Congress of Colored Parents and Teachers, which merged with the National PTA in 1970.

Government regulations are there for your own good whether you need them or not.

On February 17, 1817, in Baltimore, a city street was illuminated by gas lights for the first time in American history.

There were no great men born in my hometown—just babies.

On February 17, 1876, the first sardine was canned at Eastport, Maine. No records are available regarding the canning of the second sardine, but we assume that it was on the same day.

Peter's Leadership Principle: Success comes to those who can blow their own horn while blowing others' minds.

TEXAS SETTLEMENT DAY *February 18*

THE FRENCH EXPLORER, Robert Cavelier de La Salle, established the first settlement in Texas on February 18, 1685. La Salle also explored the Mississippi Basin, which he named Louisiana, and established France's claim to the area.

Put your money where your mouth is—lick a stamp.

On February 18, 1930, the planet Pluto was discovered by astronomer Clyde W. Tombaugh, working at the Lowell Observatory in Flagstaff, Arizona.

The federal debt limit is over 1 trillion dollars—and we call them cheap politicans.

On this day in 1953, Lucille Ball and Desi Arnaz were given an $8 million contract to continue *I Love Lucy* through the 1955 season. This was the highest single TV contract to that date.

Peter's Personality Theory: There are two kinds of losers: (1) the good loser and (2) those who can't act.

THOMAS A. EDISON received a patent for his invention, the phonograph, on February 19, 1848. This device was the beginning of the whole recording industry. Edison's assistant, John Kreusi, who constructed the first working model from the inventor's drawings, received $18.00 for his efforts.

I hate being with people who always talk about their aches and pains and medical problems—so I avoid major-league ball-players.

On February 19, 1910, "Diamond Jim" Brady's appetite showed no signs of slowing down. At a dinner party in New York, he ate seven dozen oysters, five servings of roast beef, two gallons of stewed fruit, and three gallons of orange juice.

I used to think my parents made bad decisions until I started making my own.

On February 19, 1854, Henry D. Thoreau said, "Many college textbooks which were a weariness and a stumbling block when studied, I have read a little in with pleasure and profit."

Peter's Educational Theory: Experience is the worst teacher—it gives the test before explaining the lesson.

ON FEBRUARY 20, 1962, John Glenn became the first American, and the third man, to orbit the earth in space. His vehicle was a Mercury space capsule. This day is also known as First American in Space Day.

Modern art is when you buy a picture to cover a hole in the wall and then decide that the hole looked better.

On February 20, 1809, the Supreme Court ruled that the power of the federal government is greater than that of any individual state of the Union.

There are 24 hours in a day—and only one is called the Happy Hour.

The New York City Metropolitan Museum of Art was opened February 20, 1877.

Peter's First Rule of Grammar: A double negative is a no-no.

ON FEBRUARY 21, 1804, in Mid-Glamorgan, Wales, the first self-propelled steam railway locomotive was demonstrated. It was built by Richard Trevithick and it successfully puffed along a 10-mile track carrying 70 passengers and sufficient freight to make up a total 10-ton load.

First thing Monday morning the boss said, "Have I got willpower? I haven't had a smoke since last week."

On February 21, 1885, the Washington Monument was dedicated after being under construction for 37 years. The cornerstone laying took place on July 4, 1848.

I got my girl through an act of bravery—rescued her from a lifeguard.

On February 21, 1866, Lucy B. Hobbs graduated from Ohio College of Dental Surgery to become the first woman dentist.

Peter's Postal-Delay Principle: It's not how long it takes them to handle the mail but how long it takes them to let it go that creates the problems.

WASHINGTON'S BIRTHDAY   *February 22*

GEORGE WASHINGTON, "The Father of His Country," first President of the United States of America, first in war, first in peace, first in the hearts of his countrymen, was born in Westmoreland County, Virginia, on February 22, 1732.

There is a new book just out on how to be spontaneous.

On February 22, 1879, the first "five-cent store," forerunner of the modern "five-and-ten," was opened in Utica, New York, by Frank W. Woolworth. The store was a great disappointment; its sales after a few weeks were running as low as $2.50 a day. In June 1879, Woolworth moved the store to Lancaster, Pennsylvania, where it proved a great success.

We have a family physician—he treats mine and I support his.

On February 22, 1979, the first women were allowed to register for longshore work on the piers at New York Harbor.

Peter's Conclusion: Monday is an unsatisfactory way to spend one seventh of your life.

VAUDEVILLE DAY   *February 23*

ON FEBRUARY 23, 1871, the word *vaudeville* appeared for the first time in an entertainment announcement. A traveling troupe billed as "Sargent's Great Vaudeville Company" performed for the patrons of Weisiger's Hotel in Louisville, Kentucky.

After five days at work my two days of fun is a strong-end not a weekend.

On February 23, 1905, after observing that strangers in a city were very often inhospitably received, Paul Percy Harris, a Chicago lawyer, and three friends founded the first Rotary Club.

The Surgeon General has determined that cigarette smoking can be hazardous to your health—particularly right after syphoning gas.

On February 23, 1954, the first mass inoculation with Salk polio vaccine began in Pittsburgh, Pennsylvania.

Peter's Conservation Principle: Protect all endangered species: eagles, whales, and honest politicians.

GREGORIAN CALENDAR DAY   *February 24*

POPE GREGORY XIII obtained the services of distinguished astronomers and mathematicians and assigned them the task of correcting the Julian calendar, which was ten days off at that time. On February 24, 1582, he issued a proclamation establishing the new Gregorian calendar. It is the most used calendar in the world today.

This medicine can't be habit forming—I've been taking it for years.

Mrs. Murphy's Law: Whatever can go wrong is Mr. Murphy's fault.

Upon reviewing my family's accident record, I concluded that "safe at home" applied only to baseball.

On February 24, 1868, the House of Representatives resolved to impeach President Andrew Johnson for "high crimes and misdemeanors." The Senate failed to convict him by one vote.

Peter's Staffing Principle: Many hands make light work—and heavy payrolls.

FIRST BILLION-DOLLAR CORPORATION DAY

ON FEBRUARY 25, 1901, J. P. Morgan incorporated the United States Steel Corporation, in New Jersey, creating the first billion-dollar corporation.

My latest survey shows that people don't believe in surveys.

The great opera tenor, Enrico Caruso, was born on February 25, 1873, in Naples, Italy. The city, in 1924, dedicated the world's largest candle to his memory. It measured 7 feet around and 18 feet high, is lighted annually on his birthday, and is expected to last 1,800 years.

If at first you don't succeed—failure may be your thing.

On February 25, 1836, Samuel Colt patented the six-shooter revolver.

Peter's Modern-Medicine Principle: The more effective the prescription, the more horrendous the side effects.

By an Act of Congress on February 25, 1919, Grand Canyon National Park was established in Arizona. The canyon, an immense gorge of the Colorado River, noted for its fantastic shapes and coloration, is 217 miles long, 4 to 18 miles wide from rim to rim, and has a depth of 1 mile at its maximum.

The best compliments a child can pay his parents is to set a good example for them.

The Buffalo Creek, West Virginia, flood occurred on February 26, 1972.

If you think money can't buy happiness—you're looking in the wrong catalog.

Buffalo Bill Cody, who was christened William Frederick Cody, American frontiersman and Wild West showman, was born on February 26, 1846.

Peter's Here-and-Now Principle: Live in the present—there is no better time than now to regret yesterday and fear tomorrow.

ON FEBRUARY 27, 1964, the city of Pisa asked the Italian government to spend over $1 million to straighten the 184-foot Leaning Tower of Pisa. At that time, the famous tower slanted 11 feet from the perpendicular and engineers predicted that without correction it would collapse. Reconstruction of the foundation is under way.

If you make your guests feel at home they'll wish they had stayed there.

It's no fun being sick when you don't feel well.

The prefixes pro and con have opposite meanings, as in Progress and Congress.

Ralph Nader, American attorney, consumer advocate, and author, was born on February 27, 1934.

Peter's Laugh-in Principle: When the boss tells a joke, he who laughs, lasts.

EMANCIPATION PROCLAMATION DAY

February 28

ON FEBRUARY 28, 1963, President John F. Kennedy, in a special civil-rights message to Congress, noted that in the one hundredth anniversary year of the Emancipation Proclamation, American blacks were still victims of prejudice and committed the nation to elimination of racial discrimination.

People who always agree with me are always right and I can't stand people who are always right.

On February 28, 1859, the Savannah, Georgia paper, *The Republican*, advised that a large slave auction would be held in the near future. "The Negroes will be sold in families, and be seen on the premises of Joseph Bryan in Savannah, three days prior to the day of sale, when catalogues will be furnished. . . ."

It's amazing how radical an unemployed conservative can become.

This day is also known as the U.S.S. *Princeton* Explosion Anniversary. On February 28, 1846, the new war steamer, U.S.S. *Princeton*, was cruising on the Potomac River. Aboard were President John Tyler and top officials. During a demonstration, a gun called the Peacemaker exploded, killing Abel P. Upshur, Secretary of State, Thomas W. Gilmer, Secretary of the Navy, and others.

Peter's Inevitability Principle: Live each day as if it were your last—and one of these days you'll be right.

IN SCOTLAND on February 29, 1288, Leap Year Day was established as the day when a woman could propose marriage to a man. If he refused he was required to pay a fine. This quaint custom has been replaced by the women's movement so that now women can make proposals 365 days a year and 366 days during Leap Year. This extra day is because it takes 365¼ days for the earth to orbit the sun and the four quarters make one whole day every four years.

1980 was a leap year—so was 1929.

Today, the advantage of Leap Year is that it gives you an extra day before April 15.

The universal protest sign is a stifled yawn.

Gioacchino Rossini, composer of comic operas, including *The Barber of Seville*, *Cinderella*, and *The Italian Girl in Algiers*, and many other works, was born on February 29, 1792, in Pesaro, Italy.

Peter's Cinderella Precept: People who wear glass slippers shouldn't tap-dance.

NATIONAL PIG DAY

ON THIS DATE EACH YEAR National Pig Day is observed to accord to the pig its rightful place as one of our most useful and intelligent domestic animals.

Inflation is when you live in a higher-priced neighborhood without moving.

On March 1, 1932, the 20-month-old son of Colonel and Mrs. Charles A. Lindbergh was kidnapped from his bedroom in the Lindbergh home near Hopewell, New Jersey.

National Procrastination Week starts on the first Sunday of March. Its objective is to promote the benefits of rest through postponing doing anything that doesn't have to be done today.

On March 1, 1781, the American Colonies adopted the Articles of Confederation of the United States, a prelude to the federal union.

Peter's Theory of Aging: You've reached middle age when every time you see an antique for sale you remember throwing one like that away.

THE TOLERANTS SPONSOR this observation of the birth date of the satirist Juvenal (Decimus Junius Juvenalis) who was born March 2, 60. His complaints about the inflation, crime, and politics of his time read like the gripes of today's newspapers. He wrote, "We are now suffering the evils of a long peace. Luxury, more deadly than war, broods over the city, and avenges a conquered world."

I never understood the jury system—why does it take 12 men to decide which side has the better lawyer?

On March 2, 1888, responding to the criticism that his poetry lacked meter, H. G. Wells responded, "Meters are used for gas, not the outpourings of the human heart."

At first I thought it was an abstract painting and then discovered it was a mirror.

On March 2, 1831, Thomas B. Macaulay said, "Turn where we may, within, around, the voice of great events is proclaiming to us, Reform, that you may preserve."

Peter's Movie Principle: One picture may be worth a thousand words but not $5.00 admission.

THE BILL MAKING the Star Spangled Banner the national anthem was passed by Congress and went to President Herbert Hoover for his signature on March 3, 1931. He signed the bill on the same day.

According to seismology, everything east of the San Andreas Fault will eventually plunge into the Atlantic Ocean.

On March 3, 1915, the premier of "The world's greatest silent motion picture" took place in New York. The film was David Wark Griffith's *The Birth of a Nation*.

The only thing that goes as far today as it did five years ago is the quarter that rolls under the sofa.

This is Florida Admission Day. Florida became the twenty-seventh state on March 3, 1845.

Peter's Procrastination Principle: Postponement wastes time. (More on this later.)

HOLY EXPERIMENT DAY *March 4*

ON MARCH 4, 1681, William Penn, an English Quaker, obtained from King Charles II a charter for Pennsylvania. The territory was named by the king. The royal charter, deed, and governorship were for the establishment of Penn's "Holy Experiment," a colony based on the concept of religious and political freedom. Penn spent the rest of his life developing the colony according to these principles.

I felt good when the doctor told me I was sick, because I'd hate to feel this bad if I'm well.

On March 4, 1933, Franklin Delano Roosevelt, in his inaugural address, said, "So first of all let me assert my firm belief that the only thing we have to fear is fear itself."

I wanted to join United Inflation Fighters but they raised the dues.

Abraham Lincoln, in his inaugural address, March 4, 1865, uttered these famous words, "With malice toward none, with charity for all, with firmness in the right, as God gives us to see the right."

Peter's Union Rule: The only place where the employees would go on strike to make less money is the U.S. Mint.

ON MARCH 5, 1979, the U.S. Supreme Court ruled that state laws providing that husbands, but not wives, may be required to pay alimony are unconstitutional.

It starts with puppy love and leads to a dog's life.

You can't win. I took my suit to the cleaners and even the cleaners took me to the cleaners.

On March 5, 1875, Andrew Johnson returned to the U.S. Senate, becoming the first former President to become a senator after his presidential term had expired.

Peter's Theory of Craftsmanship: The young men are too careless and the old men are too slow.

ALAMO DAY   *March 6*

TODAY IS THE ANNIVERSARY of the fall of the Texas fort, the Alamo, on March 6, 1836. The Mexican general Santa Anna led the siege that ended on March 6 when the last of the defenders was slain. General Sam Houston rallied the Texans with the war cry "Remember the Alamo," and defeated and captured Santa Anna who then signed the treaty recognizing Texas's independence.

Human survival will be achieved peace by peace.

On March 6, 1896, when Charles Brady King drove his "Horseless Carriage" on the streets of Detroit, spectators shouted, "Get a horse!" It was the first appearance of an automobile in the city that was destined to become the "Motor Capital of America."

Everybody complains about spiraling prices, but isn't that better than having them go straight up?

Michelangelo, the Italian sculptor, was born March 6, 1475, at Caprese, Tuscany.

Peter's Law of Cussedness: Anything that requires a skilled technician and is vital to the running of your household will break down on Saturday night.

ON MARCH 7, 1876, Alexander Graham Bell was issued a patent for his voice-transmission device, which he named the telephone.

Time is always running out because nobody ever heard of time running in.

On March 7, 1850, Senator Daniel Webster pleaded for the preservation of the Union in his famous "Webster's Seventh of March Speech," in which he stated, "I speak today out of a solicitous and anxious heart for the restoration to the country of that quiet harmony which makes the blessings of this Union so rich and so dear to us all. . . ."

The government fighting inflation is like the mafia fighting crime.

March 7, 1849, is Luther Burbank's Birthday. The anniversary of his birth is also observed as Bird and Arbor Day.

Peter's Accountancy Principle: Any discrepancy will not be in your favor.

THIS DAY HONORS WOMEN, particularly working women. It was proclaimed in 1910 at an international conference of women in Helsinki, Finland, ". . . that henceforth March 8 should be declared International Women's Day." This day was selected to commemorate a march and demonstration by female garment and textile workers in New York in 1857. Although this celebration originated in the United States it has been adopted internationally including in the Soviet countries.

He's a bigot—he adheres to a strict code of ethnics.

On March 8, 1894, New York State became the first state requiring dogs to be licensed.

Life is a rat race and the rats are winning.

On March 8, 1979, hundreds of thousands of Iranian women protested the edicts of Ayatollah Khomeini by chanting, "We will fight the veil."

Peter's Paradoxical Principle: Man is complex; he makes deserts bloom, and lakes die.

ON MARCH 9, 1822, in New York City, dentist Charles Graham was granted a patent for his invention of a workable set of artificial teeth.

Chicken Little only has to be right once.

On March 9, 1858, the first soda fountain, in the style of our modern-day models, was built and installed by Gustavus D. Dows in Lowell, Massachusetts.

Jack and Jill's relationship wasn't on the level.

On March 9, 1666, Samuel Pepys said, "Musick and Women I cannot but give way to, whatever my business is."

Peter's Used-Car Principle: It's hard to drive a real bargain.

ON MARCH 10, 1862, the first paper money issued by the United States government was made available in denominations of $5, $10, $20, $50, $100, $500, and $1,000.

The final test of fame is to have a crazy person think he or she is you.

On March 10, 1775, the Transylvania Company hired Daniel Boone and a group of frontiersman to clear a road through the wilderness to the Kentucky River.

Humpty Dumpty was a fall guy.

On March 10, 1876, Alexander Graham Bell transmitted the first clearly audible telephone message to his assistant in the next room, "Mr. Watson, come here, I want you."

Peter's Betting Rule: It's easy to beat the horses. Just bet more money on the winners than the losers.

JOHN CHAPMAN, better known as Johnny Appleseed, was an itinerant preacher who planted apple seeds wherever he went. He was a friend of wild animals and was regarded by the Indians as a great medicine man. He was born at Leominster, Massachusetts, September 26, 1774, and died in Allen County, Indiana, March 11, 1847.

Beggars can fill you with self-doubt. It annoys you to give to them and annoys you not to give to them.

Apple pie is not American. It was brought by the French to the Quebec trading posts long before American Independence. Apples became an American agricultural success only after Johnny Appleseed, near the end of the eighteenth century, crossed the plains planting his apple seeds.

Every time I find where it's at—they move it.

On March 11, 1873, Benjamin Disraeli uttered this timely reminder, "A university should be a place of light, of liberty and of learning."

Peter's Medication Law: Pills to be taken singly come out of the bottle in twos; those to be taken in twos come out in threes, and so on.

On March 12, 1979, movie director Alfred Hitchcock received the Life Achievement Award. He was best known for his suspenseful films. He started his career in England and in 1929 directed *Blackmail*, the first successful British talking picture. In Hollywood he made an average of one picture a year. Critics probed his films more deeply than those of any other Hollywood director. One of his trademarks was his cameo appearance in each of his films.

Arise early on Sunday morning so you can have a longer day of rest.

A home without a tree isn't fit for a dog.

George Gallup is a poll cat.

March 12 is Fireside Chat Day in recognition of President Franklin Delano Roosevelt's first Sunday evening Fireside Chat, in 1933, to the American public. He reported informally on the economic problems of the nation and on his actions to correct them.

Peter's Prediction Principle: Any year is a bad year if it begins with 19.

ON MARCH 13, 1852, in the New York *Lantern*, a cartoon by Frank Bellow showed "Uncle Sam" as the symbol of the United States for the first time. In the drawing the shipowners of Great Britain and the United States are shown in keen competition, personified as John Bull and Uncle Sam.

When in doubt, the vague generality and a fixed smile is your best ploy.

On March 13, 1925, the governor of Tennessee signed a bill making it unlawful for any teacher of the state's university or normal or public schools to teach any theory that denies divine creation as taught in the Bible.

John Doe is a nobody.

March 13 is National Be-Kind-to-Your-Amoeba Day. Its purpose is a cell-a-bration to honor nature's most famous one-cell animal.

Peter's Astrological Theory: I don't believe in astrological signs because we Virgos are very cynical.

COTTON GIN DAY *March 14*

ON MARCH 14, 1794, Eli Whitney was granted the patent on his invention, the cotton gin, a machine for separating the cotton from its seeds. This device revolutionized the cotton industry making it possible for one person to clean as much cotton in a day as 50 could previously.

The time to enjoy a foreign-travel vacation is nine days after unpacking.

Albert Einstein was born on this day in 1879 and in 1905 published his Special Theory of Relativity that revolutionized theoretical physics.

Paul Revere was an alarmist.

On March 14, 1972, *Cosmopolitan* magazine hit the stands with a centerfold featuring Burt Reynolds in a nude pose.

Peter's Attendance Principle: The bigger the crowd the more people show up for it.

THIS DAY WAS the Ides of March on the Roman calendar. It got its name from the Etruscan word that meant *to divide* because the day divided the lunar month into two equal parts. After Julius Caesar was assassinated on March 15, 44 B.C., this day came to be seen as a bad omen: "Beware the Ides of March."

A reducing pill is someone who tells you how they did it.

On March 15, 1913, only 11 days after his inauguration, President Woodrow Wilson held the first open presidential press conference in history.

The U.S. Postal Service is nothing to write home about.

March 15 is Buzzard Day in Hinckley, Ohio, when tradition says the buzzards or turkey vultures return to raise their young after wintering in the Great Smokey Mountains.

Peter's Educational Theory: Today the old phrase, "As every schoolboy knows," means nothing.

THIS DAY COMMEMORATES the first liquid-fuel-powered rocket flight which took place on March 16, 1926, at Auburn, Massachusetts. The rocket was devised by Robert Hutchings Goddard.

If ignorance is bliss, why isn't everyone smiling?

On March 16, 1830, only 31 shares of stock were traded on the New York Stock Exchange, setting a record as the slowest day in the history of the Exchange.

What this country really needs is a shopping cart with wheels that will go in the same direction.

On March 16, 1979, a movie about a nuclear-plant disaster, *The China Syndrome*, opened. It was followed a few days later by the accident at Three Mile Island, Pennsylvania.

Peter's Expediency Principle: The land and the trees be damned—what we want is fruit.

SAINT PATRICK, patron saint of Ireland, died on this day in 464. The most famous legend told of him is that he miraculously drove all the snakes and venomous creatures from the island by banging a drum. He did so well that Irish soil is still supposed to be death to any such beast that touches it. Another legend says that he used the shamrock, with its three leaves and a single stem, to illustrate the idea of the Trinity. His listeners understood and adopted the shamrock as the symbol of the land. On his deathbed he asked his friends to have a drink to ease their pain. Compliance with his last words is an explanation of the Irish predilection for whiskey.

If it weren't for underachievers, nobody could be above average.

On March 17, 1906, President Theodore Roosevelt, speaking before the members of the Gridiron Club in Washington, coined a new word, *muckrake.* The practice of muckraking, said the President, is nothing more than the deplorable habit of making sweeping and unjust charges of corruption against public officials and corporations alike.

Wallpapering is easy once you get the hang of it.

March 17 is Camp Fire Girls Founders Day, commemorating the founding of the organization and the values of its service to youth nationwide.

Peter's Pleasure Principle: Two wrongs do not make a right but it may be fun to keep trying.

CASEY JONES DAY *March 18*

ON MARCH 18, 1900, John Luther Jones, veteran engineer of the Chicago and New Orleans Limited Railway, stayed with his engine when the brakes failed, despite the certainty of a wreck. He tried to slow the hurtling brakeless express to save as many lives as possible. He died in the wreck, but his name and fame live on in the folk ballad "Casey Jones."

No person should be denied equal rights because of the shape of her skin.

The great ship *Torrey Canyon* ran aground on Seven Stones reef on this day in 1967.

The problem with taking tranquilizers is that you may find yourself being nice to people you dislike.

March 18, 1853, is the birth date of German inventor Rudolph Diesel, creator of the engine that bears his name.

Peter's Election Principle: You can fool all of the people some of the time and some of the people all of the time—and that is good enough to win the election.

SWALLOWS RETURN TO CAPISTRANO DAY

MARCH 19 IS THE LEGENDARY date for the swallows to return from Mexico to the old mission at San Juan Capistrano, California. Whenever they fail to arrive on this date, local commentators feel obliged to find an excuse. A favorite is that in olden days they were always on time, but since the San Diego Freeway was built across the path of the migrating swallows, the traffic confuses them.

Experience is what you get when you're trying for something else.

I'd rather have a splitting headache than one that is just arriving.

If at first you don't succeed, call up someone else.

On March 19, 1831, the first bank robbery in the United States took place at the City Bank of New York. The robber, Edward Smith, opened the vault with a duplicate set of keys and made off with $245,000. Later he was apprehended and sentenced to five years in Sing Sing.

Peter's Retirement Principle: You can live very well on Social Security if you managed to put a fortune aside.

VERNAL EQUINOX DAY   *March 20*

ON THIS DAY EVERY YEAR, spring begins in the northern hemisphere as the sun passes over the equator. This signifies the advent of the new year on many old calendars. It is the season in which new life arises from the winter, symbolizing the death of the old year.

I lived through the sexual revolution and never even got wounded.

On March 20, 1979, women were banned by royal decree from using hotel swimming pools in Jidda, Saudi Arabia.

Why be small and weak, when with two drinks you can be big and strong.

Uncle Tom's Cabin was published on March 20, 1857. In this story the author, Harriet Beecher Stowe, depicted the cruelty, horror, and tragedy that was possible under slavery. The first printing of 5,000 sold out in a week.

Peter's Inflation Principle: Learn to tighten your belt, because the economy is going to scare the pants off you.

ELIMINATION OF RACIAL DISCRIMINATION DAY

THIS DAY OF OBSERVANCE, officially titled International Day for the Elimination of Racial Discrimination, was initiated by the United Nations General Assembly in 1966. It is a day to remember "the victims of Sharpesville and those countless others in different parts of the world who have fallen victim to racial injustice." March 21 is the anniversary of the killing of 69 African demonstrators at Sharpesville, South Africa, in 1960.

The American Dream: Borrow $20,000 for a down payment, then an $80,000 first mortgage and a $40,000 second mortgage—and become a homeowner.

On March 21, 1843, thousands of Americans were in panic as they awaited the end of the world as predicted by William Miller, a preacher in Pittsfield, Massachusetts.

I drink to forget the price of what I'm drinking.

March 21 is Fragrance Day when we should be alert to fragrances and aware of the bouquets and perfumes of the world around us.

Peter's Voter Principle: Elections are not a gamble—in a gamble, there's a chance of winning.

BANNED IN BOSTON DAY March 22

ON MARCH 22, 1630, colonists in Boston were forbidden to gamble when a statute was adopted stipulating "that all persons whatsoever that have cards, dice, or tables in their homes shall make away with them before the next court convenes under pain of punishment."

The tough thing about making a living is that you have to do it all over again tomorrow.

On March 22, 1765, the British Stamp Act, providing that revenue stamps must be affixed to newspapers, playing cards, and legal documents, became law. The colonists resisted this unpopular legislation from the day of its enactment.

A glass of beer helps me think—two heads are better than one.

On March 22, 1954, Adlai E. Stevenson stated, "All progress has resulted from people who took unpopular positions."

Peter's Salesmanship Rule: The customer is always ripe.

MELBA TOAST DAY   *March 23*

On March 23, 1901, Dame Nellie Melba, the Australian soprano and opera star, explained how she prepared her toast. She cut the bread into very thin slices and baked them until dry and crisp. Her fans started the vogue for "Melba Toast" which later became a diet item for those trying to lose weight.

Ignorance is no excuse—it's the real thing.

On March 23, 1929, President Herbert Hoover, just 19 days in office, had a telephone installed on his desk as part of his modernization of the White House.

People who complain that we spend more on alcohol than on education just don't appreciate how much you can learn at a cocktail party.

March 23 is Liberty Day, the anniversary of Patrick Henry's 1775 speech in which he said, "I know not what course others may take, but as for me, give me liberty or give me death."

Peter's Executive Principle: Don't put off until tomorrow what your secretary can do today.

MOUNT KENNEDY
SUMMIT DAY

ON MARCH 24, 1954, Senator Robert F. Kennedy became the first person to reach the top of Mount Kennedy in the Yukon Territory. At the summit of the mountain, named by the Canadian government in honor of the late U.S. President, the senator buried a copy of his brother's 1961 inaugural address.

Horse racing and politics differ in that in horse racing the whole horse wins.

On March 24, 1959, the U.S. Court of Appeals ruled that *Lady Chatterley's Lover* by D. H. Lawrence was not an obscene book.

The bartender was so sneaky he painted the bar silver so you can't find your change.

On March 24, 1949, Walter and John Huston became the first father and son to receive Oscar awards from the Academy of Motion Picture Arts and Science, for *The Treasure of the Sierra Madre*.

Peter's Principle of Positive Thinking: I'm positive that all this optimism won't work.

ON MARCH 25, 1913, the famous Palace Theatre opened in New York. It became the headquarters of vaudeville in America and the theatre most favored by vaudeville performers. The first bill included Ed Wynn, Hy Meyer, Milton Pollock and Company, The Four Vannis, Otto Gygi, and Taylor Holmes.

There is nothing wrong with doing business with someone you don't trust—as long as you don't trust him.

On March 25, 1882, New Yorkers were fascinated by the first public demonstration of pancake making in the window of a restaurant.

The darkest hour is just before you're overdrawn.

March 25, 1867, is the birth date of the great orchestra conductor Arturo Toscanini, who once said, "I kissed my first woman and smoked my first cigarette on the same day; I have never had time for tobacco since."

Peter's Contingency Principle: When an employee finds a job he stops looking for work.

On March 26, 1937, during a local Spinach Festival, as a tribute to his well-known fondness for spinach, the residents of Crystal City, Texas, dedicated a statue to "Popeye, the Sailor," the comic-strip and animated cartoon character.

The best things in life are not free—just unexpected.

On March 26, 1925, inflation was so rampant in Italy that a public bonfire of 100 million lire in bank notes was ignited in Rome in the presence of the Minister of Finance. The bonfire was the opening event in the government's campaign to reduce the circulation of paper money.

A local villain wanted to kill his wife so he tied her to the AMTRAK rails and she starved to death.

On March 26, 1885, George Eastman manufactured the first commercial motion-picture film at his factory in Rochester, New York.

Peter's Pollution Principle: Civilization will grow on you—if you do not bathe frequently.

On March 27, 1884, the *Boston Journal* described the first long-distance telephone call: "The words were heard as perfectly as though the speakers were standing close by . . ." The call was made by the managers of the Bell Telephone Company in Boston and New York. On March 27, 1899, Guglielmo Marconi sent his first long-distance radio signals across the English Channel.

Independents of the world unite.

On March 27, 1920, movie fans went wild over the wedding of Hollywood's two most popular stars, Mary Pickford (America's Sweetheart) and Douglas Fairbanks.

Experience is what allows you to recognize a mistake when you make it again.

On March 27, 1954, Lewis Mumford, in a letter to *The New York Times*, made a strong plea to end experimentation with H-bombs. "If as a nation we have become mad, it is time for the world to take note of that madness. If we are still humane and sane, then it is time for the powerful voice of sanity to be heard once more in our land."

Peter's Fair-Play Principle: I only want to get what I deserve—unless there's an easier way.

WASHING IMPROVEMENT DAY

ON MARCH 28, 1797, Nathaniel Briggs of New Hampshire was granted a patent for a washing machine. On March 28, 1905, an issue of the *Ladies' Home Journal* advised its readers, "When planning a week's menu, consider that on washing and ironing days there will be a steady fire and select some dish that takes long slow cooking."

There are no simple solutions, only intelligent choices.

On March 28, 1921, designers predicted that American women would start to wear form-fitting, one-piece bathing suits despite "the displeasure of clergymen and Puritans alike."

We tried a waterbed but soon our marriage was drifting apart.

On this day in 1944, singing commercials were banned by radio station WQXR in New York City.

Peter's Theory of Relativity: Nepotism should be kept in the family.

ON MARCH 29, 1848, the roar of the mighty Niagara Falls stopped. The falls did not fall. A blizzard on Lake Erie caused an ice jam that blocked the Niagara River that supplied the falls. This condition lasted for 30 hours; then the ice broke and the falls were back in action.

Marriage is like the army—everyone complains, but a surprising number reenlist.

On March 29, 1867, the Act of Confederation was passed by the British Parliament, creating the Dominion of Canada, with its own federal parliament but with membership in the British Empire.

There are only three basic jokes. Since a mother-in-law is not a joke but a serious problem, and there are no father-in-law jokes, there are really only two jokes left and neither of these is funny.

March 29, 1790, is the birth date of John Tyler, tenth President of the United States. Tyler's first wife died during his term and he remarried, becoming the first President to marry while in office.

———————————————————————————

Peter's Theory of Humor: There are only three basic rules for writing humor—the only problem is that nobody knows what they are.

SINCE 1933, this day has been observed annually to honor American physicians. It is the anniversary of the first use of ether as an anesthetic during surgery, March 30, 1842, by Dr. Crawford W. Long. A red carnation is the official flower of Doctor's Day.

Today's news is too true to be good.

On March 30, 1942, a federal directive required that men's suits be manufactured without cuffs, pleats, or patch pockets for the duration of World War II.

My wife said I don't listen to her—at least I think that's what she said.

On March 30, 1858, Hyman L. Lipman of Philadelphia patented a pencil equipped with a rubber eraser.

Peter's Life Expectancy Law: Do anything long enough and it will kill you.

THIS IS THE DAY to honor the inventor of the Bunsen burner, Robert Wilhelm Eberhard von Bunsen. He provided chemists and science students with one of the most used laboratory instruments, a burner with adjustable gas and air capable of creating the most efficient flame. Bunsen was born in Germany, March 31, 1811, and became a professor of chemistry at Kessel, Marburg, Breslau, and Heidelberg.

We can wipe out colonialism but we might have to conquer the world to do it.

On March 31, 1889, the Eiffel Tower was officially opened in Paris, despite a petition of vigorous protest from 100 leading writers and artists. They claimed it was a "horrid nightmare . . . . looming over Paris like a huge black factory smokestack . . . . overwhelming our architecture." They continued, "We protest with all our might, all our indignation, in the name of French taste which is outraged."

Television is educational—before 1950 nobody knew what a headache or upset stomach looked like.

On March 31, 1796, *The North Carolina Minerva and Fayetteville Advertiser* published a manifesto stating, "Too long the male sex usurped to themselves the title of lords of creation, enacted laws and enforced statutes at large, without consulting or considering women worthy of being their co-adjustors."

Peter's Memory Rule: Tell someone they are built like an elephant and they'll never forget it.

April

Apologists for modern man's arrogant behavior have misinterpreted the idea of evolution through survival of the fittest. They have taken it to mean that life is a free-for-all struggle in which fitness is equated with aggression by tooth and claw. Survival of a species is not the result of aggression to achieve immediate advantage. It is adaptation to achieve interdependence with others. Interdependence in nature has evolved because it confers mutual benefits on the participants.

LAURENCE J. PETER,
from *The Peter Plan*

APRIL FOOL'S DAY   *April 1*

THE ORIGINS OF All Fool's Day or April Fools' Day are lost in history. In ancient Rome, this day was marked in their calendar as consecrated to fools. A celebration was arranged in which elaborate instructions had to be followed. Those who could not follow the instructions were called fools. The tradition of deceiving persons by sending them upon frivolous errands, pretending they are wanted when they are not, and betraying them into ludicrous situations, so as to call them an April Fool, is one of long standing.

A bright child is one who asks questions the teacher can answer.

On April 1, 1861, William H. Seward, Secretary of State in the new Lincoln administration, submitted to the President a memorandum, "Some Thoughts for the President's Consideration," in which he offered to take over the real operation of the government.

Few of us ever test our powers of deduction—except when filling out an income tax form.

April 1 is also Intolerance Day. The objective of this celebration is to limit intolerance to this one day. The only day it is appropriate to be prejudiced, to pontificate, to be a know-it-all is April Fool's Day.

Peter's Philosophical Principle: Everything has a natural perversity.

ON APRIL 2, 1792, the U.S. Mint was authorized to produce one-cent copper coins. Originally there were four designs struck, the "chain" cent, the "wreathed" cent, the "flowing hair" cent, and the "liberty" cent.

Neither a borrower nor a lender be—unless you are dissatisfied with your present status.

On April 2, 1792, Congress enacted legislation fixing the price of gold at $19.39 an ounce and ordered coins to be minted: Eagles, $10; Half Eagles, $5; and Quarter Eagles, $2.50.

If you watch a game, it's fun. If you play at it, it's recreation. If you work at it, it's golf.

April 2 is International Children's Book Day. This celebration, held on Hans Christian Andersen's birthday, is intended to help develop international understanding among the young through the literature of other cultures.

Peter's Teacher-Education Theory: Those that can, do. Those that can't do, teach. Those that can't teach, teach the teachers. Those that can't teach the teachers, get government grants.

On April 3, 1860, the first cross-country relay Pony Express began. Two riders, one moving east from San Francisco and the other west from St. Joseph on the Missouri River, set out to cover the 1,900 mile journey. The mail followed a route along which fresh horses and riders were available at 153 stations. This system resulted in the mail's traveling at an average rate of 12 miles per hour.

Children aren't worse today than 20 years ago—they just have better weapons.

On April 3, 1882, Jesse James, the outlaw, living under the assumed name "Thomas Howard," was shot and killed by one of his own gang members, Robert Ford.

When my son made the team, I asked him whether he preferred grass or artificial turf. He said, "I never smoked artificial turf."

April 3 is also Armenian Appreciation Day, a time for a light-hearted look at historical contributions to Armenian-American folklore.

Peter's Extraterritorial Principle: There are no signs of intelligent life in outer space, either.

THE FIRST SHOWING of *The Perils of Pauline,* one of the earliest and the most famous of all motion-picture serials, took place in New York on April 4, 1914. The serial starred Pearl White, and the first episode concluded with the announcement that future segments would feature "flying machine accidents, thrilling rescues, fires at sea, train wrecks, and automobile accidents."

Even if educational standards are deteriorating, I'm not worried because my children are all in the top 99 percent of their classes.

Dorothea Dix, who exposed the horrendous conditions existing in American insane asylums and who conducted campaigns leading to improvement of treatment of the mentally ill, was born on April 4, 1802.

I was watching the game on TV, eating peanuts, drinking beer, reading *Playboy,* and scratching the dog with my foot—and my wife accused me of doing nothing.

On April 4, 1864, Abraham Lincoln said, "I claim not to have controlled events, but confess plainly that events have controlled me."

Peter's Overweight Theory: Obesity is simply a surplus gone to waist.

POCAHONTAS'S
WEDDING DAY

ON APRIL 5, 1614, Pocahontas, daughter of the Indian Chief Powhatan, was married in Virginia to John Rolfe, an English colonist.

How is it that George Washington slept in so many places and yet never told a lie?

Martin Luther King, Jr., was assassinated on this day in 1968.

The only thing that an X-rated movie leaves to the imagination is the plot.

On April 5, 1841, Henry David Thoreau claimed, "The lament for a golden age is only a lament for golden men."

———————————————————

Peter's Tranquil Principle: Stay calm and people will suspect you don't know what's going on.

ON APRIL 6, 1906, the first animated cartoon was copyrighted. The film by James Stuart Blackton consisted of drawings of a man rolling his eyes.

She has such a warm, loving disposition—it's a shame she wastes it all on herself.

On April 6, 1957, the few remaining trolley cars in New York City made their last runs.

I would swallow my pride but I hate junk food.

On April 6, 1906, Robert E. Peary and Matthew Henson reached the North Pole in their epic adventure of discovery.

Peter's Southern-Fried Principle: A bird in the hand is finger-licking good.

THE OBSERVATION OF this day commemorates the establishment on April 7, 1948, of the World Health Organization. A special theme for health is adopted for each year.

How can I soar like an eagle when I'm working for these turkeys?

On April 7, 1927, in the auditorium of the Bell Telephone Laboratories in New York, an audience witnessed the first successful long-distance television program. Secretary of Commerce Herbert Hoover, in Washington, was seen and heard clearly by the viewers in New York.

His excuse to the policeman was "I thought the DON'T WALK signal was an ad for the bus company."

On April 7, 1775, Samuel Johnson uttered this sage observation: "Patriotism is the last refuge of a scoundrel."

Peter's Social Rule: At any social gathering, don't tell a good story—it will remind someone of a bad one.

PONCE DE LEON, in his search for the fountain of youth, landed on the coast of Florida near the present site of St. Augustine on April 8, 1513. Because the discovery occurred at the time of the Easter feast *(Pascua Florida)* he named the land La Florida and claimed it for Spain. In his quest for the fountain of youth, Ponce de Leon discovered the retirement capital of America—the fountain of old age.

If you have to ask about the cost of living—you can't afford it.

On April 8, 1946, in Geneva, the League of Nations began its final session before turning its assets and power over to the United Nations.

I remember when the air was clean and sex was dirty.

On April 8, 1913, the Seventeenth Amendment to the U.S. Constitution, requiring direct selection of senators, was ratified.

Peter's Research Principle: Most discoveries are made by mistake and the bigger the funding the longer it takes to make that mistake.

ON APRIL 9, 1865, at 1:30 P.M. General Robert E. Lee surrendered the Army of Northern Virginia to General Ulysses S. Grant. This established a federal victory, ended four years of civil war, and perpetuated the union of northern and southern states. Confederate soldiers were allowed to keep their horses and to go free to their homes, while officers were permitted the return of their swords and side arms before returning home.

Life itself is a terminal illness.

He is so weight-conscious that he takes the lint out of his navel before stepping on the scale.

Ballet dancers spend so much time on tiptoe when it would be so much simpler just to get taller dancers.

On April 9, 1928, Mae West made her New York debut in a play called *Diamond Lil*. Critics said the play was "shocking," "suggestive," and in "questionable taste." It was a great success and had a long run.

Peter's Principle of Knowledge: If you think education is expensive, try ignorance.

ON APRIL 10, 1866, Henry Bergh, a former secretary of the United States legation in St. Petersburg, Russia, after a lengthy effort, succeeded in obtaining recognition for the humane society when the New York legislature granted a charter for the American Society for the Prevention of Cruelty to Animals.

They're the perfect couple—she's a hypochondriac and he's a pill.

On April 10, 1849, Walter Hunt of New York City received a patent for his invention of the safety pin.

We went to a movie for the whole family—to walk out on.

On April 10, 1829, William Booth, founder of the Salvation Army, was born in Nottingham, England.

Peter's Late Law: People who are late are always in a better mood than those who have to wait for them.

THIS DAY COMMEMORATES the founding of the Society for the Preservation and Encouragement of Barber Shop Quartet Singing in America (SPEBSQSA), which took place in Tulsa, Oklahoma, on April 11, 1938.

Retirement can be difficult—just because you're put out to pasture doesn't mean you're in clover.

On April 11, 1947, for the first time in baseball history, a black player appeared with a major-league team. The player was Jackie Robinson who joined the Brooklyn Dodgers in an exhibition game with the New York Yankees.

I had so little trust in our congressman that when he admitted he had lied—I didn't believe him.

On April 11, 1931, Dorothy Parker retired as drama critic for *The New Yorker*, ending her self-described "Reign of Terror."

Peter's Expectation Principle: The word *tax* comes from the Latin *taxare*, meaning "to touch sharply," so what can you expect?

MAN IN SPACE DAY April 12

ON APRIL 12, 1961, Yuri Gagarin became the first man in space. In the space vehicle *Vostok I*, launched by the USSR, he orbited the earth in 108 minutes. Prediction: The space program will go far.

If the world is getting smaller, why does postage keep going up?

Beginning on April 12, 1938, anyone applying for a marriage license in the state of New York would henceforth have to submit to a blood test for syphilis.

Conscience is that still small voice that tells you that the IRS might audit your return.

On April 12, 1861, civil war came to the United States as Confederate forces under the command of General P. T. Beauregard opened fire on Fort Sumter in South Carolina. The first shot was fired by a 67-year-old Virginian, Edmund Ruffin.

Peter's Eternal Rules: Don't expect much of a country in which half of the people are below average.

ON APRIL 13, 1958, to the cheers and applause of an audience of enthusiastic Moscow music lovers, 23-year-old Van Cliburn from Kilgore, Texas, was awarded the first prize in the Soviet Union's Tchaikovsky International Piano Contest.

If the truth doesn't hurt, what is it I feel when I do my income tax?

On April 13, 1964, Sidney Poitier became the first black to win a top motion-picture Oscar when he was named the best actor of 1963 at the annual ceremonies.

A fine is a tax for doing bad; a tax is a fine for doing good.

A Presidential Proclamation established that Thomas Jefferson's Birthday will be observed on April 13 each year.

Peter's Taxation Principle: Build a better mousetrap and the government will build a better mousetrap tax.

MEETINGS STARTING in 1826 between representatives of some or all of the independent states of the Western Hemisphere (Canada was usually excluded) led to formation of the International Union of American Republics in 1890. The name was later changed to Pan American Union. It dealt with common defense and jurisdictional matters, such as financial and territorial claims, extradition of criminals, international law, copyrights and patents, and status of aliens. On May 28, 1930, by Presidential Proclamation, April 14 was established as Pan American Day.

Collecting things is a waste of effort when you consider how things collect on their own.

On April 14, 1828, the first edition of Noah Webster's dictionary was published.

How can they call it an increase in the cost of living when the price of cemetery plots goes up?

On April 14, 1865, at Ford's Theatre in Washington, D.C., President Abraham Lincoln was shot. He died the following day.

Peter's Egalitarian Principle: If you can't keep up with the Joneses, drag them down to your level.

ON APRIL 15, 1923, insulin, which had been discovered in 1922 by Dr. Frederick Banting of Toronto, Canada, became available for general use in the treatment of diabetes.

One thing death has over taxes—death doesn't get worse.

On April 15, 1900, laborers working on the new Cornell Dam at Croton, New York, went out on strike in protest over current wage rates. The strikers were demanding a raise from their present daily wage of $1.25 to $1.50.

One thing I don't like about the Internal Revenue Service is that it is more concerned about how I spend my money than how the government spends my money. Whatever you think of bureaucracy, you've got to hand it to the IRS.

April 15 is Income Tax Day, the day the *Titanic* sank, and the day Lincoln died.

Peter's Taxation Principle: In April your salary will go to four figures—1040.

ON APRIL 16, 1905, Andrew Carnegie put $10 million in the hands of five distinguished men. The income from this fund was to be used for pensions for retired college and university professors. The fund became the Carnegie Foundation for the Advancement of Teaching.

The difference between last year's taxes and this year's taxes is the difference between being sheared and skinned.

On April 16, 1862, Congress abolished slavery in the District of Columbia and appropriated $100,000 to be paid to District slaves wishing to emigrate to Liberia or Haiti.

Why is it that with all the shortages we still have a litter problem?

Charlie Chaplin (Charles Spencer Chaplin), the great motion-picture comedian, was born in London, England, April 16, 1889.

Peter's Genealogy Principle: You can trace the roots of your family tree, but be forewarned you may find plenty of sap in the branches.

VERRAZANO DAY   *April 17*

THIS DAY CELEBRATES the discovery of New York Harbor by Giovanni Verrazano, a Florentine navigator, on April 17, 1524. He explored the coast of North America from Cape Fear, North Carolina, to Cape Breton, Nova Scotia, and was the first European to sight New York and Narragansett bays.

There's a new way to reduce your bills—it's called microfilm.

On April 17, 1944, the manpower shortage was so acute that a restaurant owner in Seattle, Washington, desperately in need of a woman dishwasher, advertised: "Woman wanted to wash dishes. Will marry if necessary."

Everybody talks about the weather but I do something about it—I stay inside.

On April 17, 1897, Thornton Wilder, American novelist, was born.

Peter's Adviser Principle: A consultant is an unemployed practitioner.

AT 10 P.M. on April 18, 1775, Paul Revere and William Dawes started out to warn American patriots, from Boston to Concord, of the approaching British. This mission has become known as "The Midnight Ride of Paul Revere," and is generally regarded as the beginning of the American Revolution.

I found that the boss is not a bad guy—unless you get to know him.

April 18, 1934, began the era of the Laundromat when the first "Washateria" was opened in Forth Worth, Texas.

Inflation is when nobody has enough money because everybody has too much.

On April 18, 1906, the center of the city of San Francisco was destroyed by an earthquake and the fire that followed.

Peter's Civil Service Rule: Start slow and taper off.

CHARLES E. DURYEA DAY   *April 19*

ON APRIL 19, 1892, Charles E. Duryea of Springfield, Massachusetts, after working for eight months on his horseless carriage, took it out of his shop for a successful drive. Duryea's vehicle, the first American-made automobile, was named by its builder a "buggyaut."

A fanatic is one who would be an idealist if he happened to be on your side.

On April 19, 1933, the United States abandoned the gold standard.

The happiest parents are those without children.

Duke Antonio Fernando, ruler of Guastalla in Italy, never drank because a fortune-teller warned that alcohol would kill him. On April 19, 1729, the duke rubbed his sore muscles with alcohol, caught fire, and burned to death.

Peter's Folk Medicine: The best home remedy is just being there.

ON APRIL 20, 1902, Marie and Pierre Curie isolated one gram of radium salts from eight tons of pitchblende and determined the atomic weight and properties of radium and polonium

You're only young once—after that you need other excuses.

Adolf Hitler was born on this day in 1889.

You ought to be on the stage—and there's one due any minute.

On April 20, 1947, famous radio comedian Fred Allen was cut off the air in the middle of his show because of a joke about a mythical network vice president.

Peter's Guaranteed Reducing Plan: Only eat when the news is good.

ON APRIL 21, 1895, Woodville Latham presented a demonstration of the projection of a motion picture on a screen in New York City.

I hate intolerant people.

On April 21, 1940, the phrase "The sixty-four-dollar-question" became a part of the American idiom when it was used for the first time on a radio quiz program, *Take It or Leave It*.

We're equipped three ways to have all the answers—we've got an encyclopedia, a home computer, and a teenager.

On April 21, 1938, Franklin D. Roosevelt presented Americans with this important reminder: "Remember, remember always that all of us, and you and I especially, are descended from immigrants and revolutionists."

Peter Pan Principle: Marriages either pan out or peter out.

EARTH DAY *April 22*

THE FIRST EARTH DAY was observed April 22, 1970, with celebrations focusing on the need to reclaim the purity of the air, water, and living environment. The motto was "Give Earth a Chance." The U.S. Environmental Protection Agency participated in the tenth anniversary celebration, April 22, 1980. Although this date has seen the largest celebrations, Earth Day is observed by a number of groups on various dates.

My problem is I say what I'm thinking before I think what I'm saying.

On April 22, 1864, Congress authorized the director of the Mint to use the motto "In God We Trust" on all coins of the United States. The motto was proposed originally by a clergyman, the Reverend M. R. Watkinson.

To a taxpayer, everything Congress calls a bill—is.

On April 22, 1348, at a royal ball in England, the Countess of Salisbury was dancing with King Edward III when one of her garters slipped off. The king retrieved it and put it on his leg. This was the beginning of the Order of the Garter, the highest order of English knighthood.

Peter's Theory of Locomotion: Travel has improved greatly but most places we go to have deteriorated.

SAINT GEORGE'S FEAST DAY   *April 23*

SAINT GEORGE, patron saint of England, became a martyr on April 23, 303, when he was beheaded for complaining to the emperor about his severe and bloody edicts. He was the hero of the Saint George and the Dragon legend. The dragon demanded daily live sacrifices to satisfy its appetite. When the king's daughter became its next intended victim, Saint George's faith enabled him to slay the vicious creature. In 1334 at the Feast of Saint George, the Noble Order of Saint George was created.

I went to a singles bar—but I still ordered doubles.

On April 23, 1949, Governor Adlai E. Stevenson of Illinois vetoed a bill that would require cats to be leashed. "I cannot agree that it should be the declared public policy of Illinois that a cat visiting a neighbor's yard or crossing the highway is a public nuisance. It is in the nature of cats to do a certain amount of unescorted roaming. . . . In my opinion, the state of Illinois and its local governing bodies already have enough to do without trying to control feline delinquency. . . ."

My ambition is to die young—but at an advanced age.

Peter's Administrative Rule: If a program isn't working, expand it.

THE LIBRARY OF CONGRESS, the national library of the United States, was established in Washington on April 24, 1800, when Congress voted $5,000 for the purchase of books for the use of its members.

The logician's will read: "Being of sound mind and body, how come I am dead?"

On April 24, 1897, William W. Price reported to work at *The Washington Star*, becoming the first journalist to be known as the "White House reporter."

My wife doesn't understand me—I sympathize with her; neither do I.

On April 24, 1945, delegates of 46 nations met in San Francisco to plan the organization of a permanent United Nations.

Peter's Basic Law of Budgets: You can only spend it once.

MARCONI DAY   *April 25*

GUGLIELMO MARCONI, the inventor of the wireless telegraph, the forerunner of radio, television, and modern telecommunication, was born on April 25, 1874, at Bologna, Italy.

Dullness is in the eye of the beholder.

On April 25, 1901, New York became the first state requiring automobile owners to have license plates for their vehicles.

I discovered why he accomplishes so little—he's a restaholic.

On April 25, 1812, Thomas Jefferson stated these important words: "We believe that the just standing of all nations is the health and security of all."

Peter's Principle of Patronage: A politican is known by the company that keeps him.

ON APRIL 26, 1880, Mr. Fleuss, the inventor of the "submarine diving dress" remained for two hours under water at the Westminster Aquarium in London. He claimed that he could stay under water for five hours without inconvenience and enjoy perfect freedom of movement.

As I understand our foreign policy, we will sell fighter planes, missiles, tanks, guns, bombs, and flamethrowers only to countries promising to use them for peaceful purposes.

On April 26, 1865, federal troops discovered the hiding place of John Wilkes Booth—the tobacco barn on the farm of Richard Garrett near Port Royal, Virginia. When Lincoln's assassin refused to surrender, a soldier shot and killed him, despite orders to take him alive.

My teenage son is wasting time studying economics—what could a schoolteacher know about money?

On April 26, 1954, the nationwide test of Salk polio vaccine began in the United States.

Peter's Television Law: If it moves, the public will watch it.

CANADA-UNITED STATES UNFORTIFIED BORDER DAY

ON APRIL 27, 1817, the Rush-Bagot Agreement between the United States and Canada, providing for maintenance of an undefended border between the two countries, was signed. It was ratified by the U.S. Senate April 16, 1818.

My doctor told me to slow down—but I couldn't get a job at the post office.

On April 27, 1947, baseball fans everywhere observed Babe Ruth Day. The largest observance was at Yankee Stadium, where 58,339 persons gave the seriously ill "Sultan of Swat" the greatest ovation in the history of the national pastime.

Live, love, and enjoy each day—none of us came with a guarantee but we all have an expiration date.

On April 27, 1937, the U.S. Social Security system made its first benefit payment.

Peter's Security Principle: The only way to assure that your bread will land jelly side up is to put jelly on both sides.

ON APRIL 28, 1789, while the British naval vessel *Bounty*, under the command of Captain William Bligh, was transporting breadfruit trees from the Society Islands to the West Indies, the crew led by Fletcher Christian mutinied. They put Captain Bligh and 18 others in a small open boat and set them adrift. Bligh was an outstanding navigator and sailor and managed to row 3,600 miles to the nearest island and get back to England. The mutineers established a successful colony on Pitcairn Island. The story of the Mutiny on the Bounty has been the basis of popular books and movies.

The cave dweller's wife complained that he hadn't dragged her anywhere in months.

On April 28, 1937, a new feature was added to the attractions of the Great White Way in New York when Douglas Leigh introduced the first electrical animated cartoon on the front of a building in Times Square.

I never entertain wicked thoughts—but sometimes they entertain me.

April 28, 1919, at Dayton, Ohio, Mr. Irwin parachuted to safety, performing the first successful parachute jump.

Peter's Value Principle: The best things in life aren't things.

ON APRIL 29, 1913, inventor Gideon Sundback of Hoboken, New Jersey, patented what he called a "separable fastener." He had invented the all-purpose zipper that has made changes in our clothing and many other products affecting our daily lives.

I don't want a cheaper car—I want an expensive car that costs less.

A used car is all right as far as it goes.

I explained to the young lady that I needed her number because I was writing a telephone book.

On April 29, 1894, Coxey's Army of unemployed, led by Jacob S. Coxey, arrived in Washington, D.C., to petition for relief legislation. After a demonstration on the steps of the Capitol, Coxey and some of his chief aides were arrested for "walking on the grass" and sentenced to 20 days in jail.

Peter's Real-Estate Principle: The most beautiful home ever built cannot stand if the land is suitable for a supermarket, office, or condominium.

ON APRIL 30, 1789, George Washington was inaugurated in New York as President of the United States. A great crowd assembled to watch the first President of the United States take the oath of office. Washington was sworn in on the balcony of Federal Hall by Chancellor Robert R. Livingston. The crowd broke into a great cheer, a 13-gun salute sounded from the harbor, and a flag was raised above the building.

Before you decide to retire, take a week off and watch daytime television.

On April 30, 1803, the United States more than doubled its size by the Louisiana Purchase in which it acquired from France all of its territory west of the Mississippi River for about $15 million or approximately 4 cents an acre.

Some days the only good things on TV are the vase and the clock.

On April 30, 1954, Bernard M. Baruch made this optimistic statement: "There are no such things as incurables; there are only things for which man has not found a cure."

Peter's Law of Supply and Demand:
(1) If you need it, you will have just thrown it away.
(2) If you throw it away, you will soon need it.

THE FIRST DAY OF MAY has been celebrated since ancient times. The origin of European May Day lies in the Roman Feast of Flowers. Early in the morning young men and women gathered flowers to decorate their houses and the maypole for the day of feasting, dancing, and singing. Spring festivals and maypoles are still common, but in 1880 it became a workers' day in the United States. Today it is widely observed in socialist countries as a worker's holiday and a time for demonstrations.

Smog is a combination of exhaust fumes, smoke, fog, and legislative inaction.

On May 1, 1884, in Chicago, construction started on a ten-story office building, the first structure to be called a "skyscraper." On May 1, 1931, the Empire State Building was dedicated. The new skyscraper was 102 stories.

This month we honor cooks, waitresses, nurses, teachers, counselors—or to use their generic name, Mothers.

By Presidential Proclamation, May 1 is also Law Day and Loyalty Day in the United States.

Peter's Law of Statistical Probability: There are only a few ways of doing a thing right, but the ways of doing a thing wrong are infinite.

ROBERT'S RULES DAY   *May 2*

MAY 2 is the anniversary of the birth in 1837 of Henry Martyn Robert, author of *Robert's Rules of Order*. Robert graduated from the U.S. Military Academy at West Point and was commissioned in the Corps of Engineers, retiring with the rank of brigadier general. When he presided over a chaotic meeting of his church, he became interested in the fact that there was no generally accepted set of parliamentary rules. He wrote his own code, and its publication became a commercial success. His original book and subsequent publications became the standard parliamentary guides.

I'm always impressed by persons who can speak several languages—or keep their mouth shut in one.

They said the explosion was caused by the boiler being empty and the engineer being full.

It's when we forget ourselves that we do the memorable.

May 2, 1904, was the birth date of Harry Lillis (Bing) Crosby, popular singer and actor.

Peter's Rule of Predictable Change: A year of bad results is invariably followed by a year of worse results.

ON MAY 3, 1919, America's first passenger airline service began when pilot Robert Hewitt took off from New York City with passengers—Mrs. Hoagland and Miss Hodges—bound for Atlantic City, New Jersey.

Middle age is when it takes longer to rest than to get tired.

On May 3, 1963, thousands of blacks, including many school children, staged a two-day protest march in Birmingham, Alabama. The city's police commissioner, Eugene (Bull) Connor, ordered the marchers to be set upon by police dogs or to be sent sprawling by powerful jets of water from fire hoses. By the end of the day 2,500 adults and juveniles were held in local jails.

There has been a bumper crop of collisions this year.

On May 3, 1971, national noncommercial network radio began programming, financed by the Corporation for Public Broadcasting.

Peter's Postulate: The universal aptitude for ineptitude makes any human accomplishment incredible.

MANHATTAN PURCHASE DAY   *May 4*

ON MAY 4, 1626, Governor Peter Minuit brought over four shiploads of settlers and 300 cattle and bought 20,000 acres of land—the entire island of Manhattan. He paid the Indians $24.00 worth of scarlet cloth and brass buttons for the island.

Statistics show that by the age of 75 there are three women to one man—what a time for a man to get those odds.

On May 4, 1961, the first of the so-called "Freedom Riders," a biracial group of 13 persons, set out by bus from Washington, D.C., bound for New Orleans, to test segregation barriers in interstate buses and terminals.

Middle age is when work is a lot less fun and fun is a lot more work.

May 4 is Students' Memorial Day in memory of four students killed by National Guardsmen during antiwar demonstrations at Kent State University, Ohio, in 1970, and of all students martyred in the cause of human rights.

Peter's Probability Law: You can't win them all, but you can lose them all.

ON MAY 5, 1862, at the Battle of Puebla, the outnumbered Mexican troops under General Ignacio Zaragoza defeated the invading French forces of Napoleon III. The anniversary of the victory is a Mexican national holiday and is observed by Mexicans everywhere with festivals, parades, dances, and speeches.

The police strike caused the criminal a real problem—he wanted to give himself up but refused to cross the picket line.

On May 5, 1904, Cy Young of the Boston Red Sox pitched a perfect no-hit, no-run game against the Philadelphia Americans, during which no man reached first base. Young played in the major leagues for 22 years and won more games—511—and pitched more games—906—than any other pitcher.

The person who stays late at the office may not be working—he just may not want to go home.

On May 5, 1925, John T. Scopes, a biology teacher in the public-school system of Dayton, Tennessee, was arrested for teaching the theory of evolution.

Peter's Theory of Labor Statistics: An "acceptable level of unemployment" is a percentage established by a person who still has a job.

REFRIGERATION DAY   *May 6*

ON MAY 6, 1851, Dr. John Farrie of New Orleans patented a "mechanical refrigeration machine" that produced a frigid temperature by compressing air in a cylinder immersed in a chamber of cooling water.

Sending my son to college was a valuable educational move—it taught me self-denial.

On May 6, 1856, Sigmund Freud, the father of psychoanalysis, was born in Freiberg, Moravia.

When I wanted a raise the boss told me the job was unimportant, but when I wanted a day off the job was too important.

On May 6, 1926, when George Bernard Shaw was asked if he agreed with Sinclair Lewis's refusal of the Pulitzer Prize, he replied, "I don't agree with anything."

Peter's Gossip Principle: Always keep a secret—for an appreciative audience.

THE TELSTAR COMMUNICATIONS SATELLITE was launched in 1962, inaugurating a new age of electronic communications. It was designed to amplify a signal received from an earth station and relay it back to another earth station. It was launched by rocket and powered by batteries charged by solar cells. Minutes after launching, the first television pictures were transmitted across the Atlantic and received in England and France. Telephone, telegraph, telephoto and other transmissions were also made. After four months of successful operation, command decoders failed, probably affected by radiation from the Van Allen belt. On May 7, 1963, Telstar 2, an even more successful, more durable, and heavier satellite was launched into a higher orbit.

The United States has the strangest foreign policy—based on exchanging American dollars for bad will.

On May 7, 1824, Ludwig van Beethoven's Ninth Symphony was presented for the first time.

Our landing on the moon was a big success—the moon was uninhabited, thus saving us millions in foreign aid.

On May 7, 1915, during World War I, the British ocean liner *Lusitania* was sunk by a German submarine.

Peter's Hangover Theory: This morning's pain occupies the same space in the head that was not used last night.

MISSISSIPPI RIVER DISCOVERY DAY

ON MAY 8, 1541, Hernando de Soto, with his band of Spanish explorers, discovered the Mississippi River at a point near the present city of Memphis, Tennessee.

My daughter and her mother don't see eye-to-eye—my daughter wants to find a nice man and settle down and her mother wants her to get married.

On May 8, 1958, during a goodwill tour of South America, Vice President and Mrs. Richard M. Nixon were greeted with hostility in Peru. In Lima a crowd of 2,000 pelted him with fruit and eggs, and stones were thrown. Later the Nixons were spat upon as they entered their hotel.

When I was young there was no respect for youth. Now there's no respect for age. I missed it coming and going.

On May 8, 1911, England signed a treaty with China that made opium the main trading commodity with the Chinese.

Peter's Small-Print Principle: Education is what you get from reading the small print. Experience is what you get from not reading it.

ON MAY 9, 1754, Benjamin Franklin published the first American cartoon. It appeared in his *Pennsylvania Gazette* and was titled "Join or Die." It showed a snake cut into pieces with each piece representing one of the states.

I wrote to the postmaster about how to improve the service—but the letter was lost in the mail.

On May 9, 1926, U.S. Navy Commander Richard E. Byrd and Floyd Bennett became the first men to fly over the North Pole.

He made a killing in the market—shot his broker.

On May 9, 1914, President Wilson issued a proclamation that the second Sunday in May be dedicated as a "public expression of our love and reverence for the mothers of this country."

Peter's Persistence Principle: The admirable firmness in ourselves is detestable stubbornness in others.

GOLDEN SPIKE DAY   *May 10*

THIS DAY IS THE ANNIVERSARY of the May 10, 1869, completion of the first transcontinental railway, when the Union Pacific and the Central Pacific railways met at Promontory Point, Utah. To celebrate the event, Leland Stanford, president of the Central Pacific, drove in a golden spike—missing the first stroke.

The good thing about my wife's joining Women's Lib is that she now complains about all men—not just me.

On May 10, 1872, Victoria Woodhull became the first female candidate for the United States presidency when she was nominated by the National Equal Rights Party.

The best way to prove that crime doesn't pay would be to let the government run it.

On May 10, 1930, the first planetarium in the United States was opened in Chicago, Illinois.

Peter's Election Principle: Success comes to those who can keep things under their hat while tossing it into the ring.

ON MAY 11, 1752, at a meeting of the Board of Directors of the Philadelphia Contributionship for Insurance of Houses from Loss of Fire, a seal was adopted for the company—four hands united—and the issuing of fire-insurance policies was ordered. Board members included James Hamilton, the Lieutenant Governor, and Benjamin Franklin. The first policy was issued to John Smith, the company treasurer, who wrote his own policy in which it cost him one pound to insure his house for 1,000 pounds.

Nothing is impossible to the executive who doesn't have to do it himself.

A problem with democracy is that when a congressman gets up to speak he says nothing, nobody listens, and then everybody disagrees.

Confucius say, "He who shoot off mouth, often lose face."

Irving Berlin, the composer of hundreds of popular songs and many successful shows, was born on May 11, 1888.

Peter's Principle of Optimal Committee Size: A committee should consist of an odd number and three is too many.

FLORENCE NIGHTINGALE DAY

THE ENGLISH NURSE WHO, through her devotion to her calling, did more than any other single person to develop modern nursing procedures and to elevate the status of nursing as a profession, was born in Florence, Italy, on May 12, 1820. She founded the Nightingale School for Nurses and was author of *Notes on Nursing*. Her efforts to ease the suffering of the wounded soldiers in the Crimea inspired Henry Wadsworth Longfellow to write "Santa Filomina" which contained these lines: "The speechless sufferer turns to kiss / Her shadow, as it falls / Upon the darkening walls."

Hear no evil, see no evil, speak no evil—and you'll be a flop at the cocktail party.

An economist is a person who knows more about money than the people who have it.

You can never get much done unless you go ahead and do it before you are ready.

On May 12, 1978, the National Oceanic and Atmospheric Administration, responding to pressure from women's groups, announced it would begin naming Pacific storms after men.

Peter's Committee Principle: You can get the group together any time they're on an expense account.

CASEY AT THE BAT DAY *May 13*

ON MAY 13, 1888, the actor De Wolfe Hopper recited the poem "Casey at the Bat" during the second act of *Prince Methusalem,* a musical comedy that was playing at Wallack's Theatre in New York. When Hopper finished the whole audience rose from its seats and broke into a cheer. Ernest L. Thayer's poem became an overnight success, and Hopper's reading of it became a part of every show he appeared in. Toward the end of his career he estimated that he had recited it 15,000 times.

It's a delicate balance. If you drive too fast you could wreck the front of your car, and if you drive too slow you could wreck the back of your car.

On May 13, 1916, Sholem Aleichem, considered by many to be the greatest Jewish humorist, died in New York. His dying wish was that Jews the world over, in moments of depression, would think of him and laugh. The sole specification for attendance at his annual May 13 memorial service is that laughter must dominate the ceremony.

The problem with hitting the jackpot on a slot machine is that it takes so long to put the money back in.

On May 13, 1607, the first colonists to establish a permanent English settlement in the New World landed near the James River in Virginia and started to build their fortress community, the beginning of Jamestown.

Peter's Antique Rule: If anything is so old nobody knows what to do with it, the price goes up.

SMALLPOX VACCINATION DAY

ON MAY 14, 1796, in England, Edward Jenner proved that a vaccine made from the blood of a cow infected with cowpox could be used safely and effectively on human beings in inoculating them against smallpox. He experienced much opposition to his system of immunization, much of it from the medical profession, but fortunately, vaccination was eventually accepted. This once-common disease has been virtually eliminated.

Time is relative—it depends on which side of the bathroom door you're on.

On May 14, 1913, John D. Rockefeller's donation of $100 million, said to be the largest *single* gift of money to date, established the Rockefeller Foundation for the promotion of the "well-being of mankind throughout the world."

An egotist is a stupid person who thinks he knows as much as you do.

On May 14, 1853, Gail Borden applied for a patent for the process of making condensed milk.

Peter's Cooperation Principle: Diplomacy is doing with a smile that which you have to do anyway.

PEACE OFFICERS MEMORIAL DAY

BY PRESIDENTIAL PROCLAMATION, May 15 each year is Peace Officers Memorial Day, a time to honor police officers generally and particularly to pay tribute to those who have lost their lives in the line of duty.

Admitting a mistake to my mother-in-law is like bleeding in front of a shark.

May 15 is Straw Hat Day in America, the day considered by many fashion-conscious men as the official date on which it is permissible to start wearing straw hats for the summer season.

To be a success socially one must be prepared to learn many things one already knows.

On May 15, 1940, the first nylon stockings were sold in America.

Peter's Safe-Driving Rule: Beware of the irresponsible, reckless speeder—especially if it's you.

ON MAY 16, 1866, the United States five-cent piece was authorized. This coin has always been referred to as a "nickel," although it is composed of 25 percent nickel and 75 percent copper.

If you think you cannot change the past, you've never read an obituary.

On May 16, 1927, despite the fact that the manufacture and sale of alcoholic beverages was unlawful, the Supreme Court ruled that "bootleggers" must file income-tax forms.

When approaching a school always watch out for children—they tend to be dangerous drivers.

On May 16, 1929, the first Oscar awards by the Academy of Motion Picture Arts and Sciences were presented in Los Angeles.

Peter's Competence Rule: If you can tell the difference between good advice and bad advice you don't need advice.

ON MAY 17, 1899, the first Western movie was copyrighted. The movie, made by the Edison Company, was *Cripple Creek Bar Room*.

A super salesman is one who tells a woman it's a bargain and a man that it's deductible.

On May 17, 1792, 24 New York brokers met under a buttonwood tree on the present site of 68 Wall Street and signed an agreement to fix uniform rates of commission for the sale of stocks and bonds. This was the beginning of the New York Stock Exchange.

An antique isn't always as old as it's cracked up to be.

On May 17, 1875, the first Kentucky horse race was held at Churchill Downs, Louisville, Kentucky.

Peter's Automotive-Safety Principle: The degree of failure of an automobile braking system is in direct ratio to the percentage grade upon which the vehicle is traveling.

WORLD GOODWILL DAY   *May 18*

MAY 18 is observed as a special day to work for peace in a world where every day should be devoted to peace. It is the anniversary of the opening of the first Hague Peace Conference, May 18, 1899.

I knew I was getting older when I realized I was spending more time talking to the druggist than to the bartender.

There are a lot of things money can't buy—for example, what it bought last year.

The way to find what's up—is to go shopping.

May 18 is also Visit Your Relative Day, a time to renew family ties and experience the joys of visiting often-thought-of-seldom-seen relatives.

_____

Peter's Experiential Principle: Old folks know more about being young than young folks know about being old.

ON MAY 19, 1928, 51 frogs were entered in the Jumping Frog Jubilee at Angels Camp, Calaveras County, California. The judges selected as the winner The Pride of San Joaquin, a frog owned by L. R. Fischer of Stockton, California. The frog jumped 3 feet, 4 inches. This event is held annually to commemorate Mark Twain's story, "The Celebrated Jumping Frog of Calaveras County."

Inflation is when it's easier to make money than to make a living.

You have to believe in luck—or how are you going to explain the success of people you don't like?

I only use the air-conditioning during the months with no R in them.

On May 19, 1879, Nancy Witcher Langhorne, was born in Virginia. In 1919, as Lady Astor, she became the first woman to sit in the British Parliament.

Peter's Communication Principle: In human relations the easiest thing to achieve is a misunderstanding.

ELIZA DOOLITTLE DAY

May 20

THE PURPOSE OF THIS DAY is to honor Miss Eliza Doolittle, the heroine of George Bernard Shaw's play *Pygmalion*, for exemplifying the importance of speaking one's native language properly.

If you live correctly you might be able to achieve senility in perfect health.

At 7:40 A.M. on May 20, 1927, Charles A. Lindbergh took off in his monoplane, the *Spirit of St. Louis*, from Roosevelt Field, New York, in an attempt to win a $25,000 prize for the first nonstop flight across the Atlantic.

Don't despair if all your dreams come out wrong—you could have a great career as an economic forecaster.

On May 20, 1978, Mavis Hutchison, 53, jogged into New York City to become the first woman to run across America—3,000 miles in 69 days, averaging 45 miles a day.

Peter's Instructional Principle: Teaching is the art of understanding people who don't explain things very well and explaining things to people who don't understand very well.

LINDBERGH DAY

May 21

THIS DAY WE CELEBRATE the anniversary of the first solo transatlantic flight from New York to Paris by Charles A. Lindbergh in the airplane *Spirit of St. Louis,* March 21, 1927. His plane, upon takeoff, was stocked with 451 gallons of gasoline and 20 gallons of oil, but had no lights, heat, radio, deicing equipment, or automatic controls. The crossing took 33½ hours and received more press coverage than any other single event in history. American papers devoted 27,000 columns of words to reporting the story.

We all start things we can't finish—but you're really incompetent when you start things you can't even begin.

On May 21, 1957, thirty years later to the day, Major Robinson Risnor, U.S. Air Force, retraced Lindbergh's solo nonstop flight across the Atlantic. It took him 6 hours, 38 minutes.

You don't need to take a person's advice to make him feel good—just ask for it.

On May 21, 1881, Clara Barton founded the American Red Cross in Washington, D.C.

Peter's Poll Principle: Public opinion is what people think other people are thinking.

MARITIME DAY CELEBRATES the anniversary of the day a steamship first set out to cross the Atlantic from Savannah, Georgia, to Liverpool, England: the steamship *Savannah* on May 22, 1819. National Maritime Day is observed annually by Presidential Proclamation.

Free advice is the kind that costs you nothing—unless you use it.

On May 22, 1868, members of the Reno Gang committed "The Great Train Robbery." They first held up the crew of the Indianapolis-bound Jefferson, Madison, and Indianapolis train at Marshfield, Indiana. After overpowering the crew, the masked robbers detached the locomotive and the adjoining Adams Express car and sped to a spot outside of Seymour, Indiana, where they made off with $98,000 in cash from a safe in the express car.

Mother Nature giveth—Father Time taketh away.

Richard Wagner, the great German opera composer, was born on May 22, 1813.

Peter's Confidence Rule: Success is doing what you do well and letting others do everything else.

BIFOCALS DAY is observed on the anniversary of Benjamin Franklin's writing about his new invention, the bifocal eye-glasses. He wrote, "I have only to move my eyes up and down as I want to see distinctly far or near."

Advice is counsel given by someone who can't use it to someone who won't.

On May 23, 1904, European steamship companies transporting immigrants to the United States announced they would reduce their steerage rates to $10 a person.

You've reached the difficult age when you're too tired to work and too poor to quit.

May 23 is also Kirtland's Warbler Day, a time to promote survival of the 200 existing pairs of Kirtland Warblers. On May 23, 1851, the first of these birds was taken for study on the farm of Dr. Jaren Kirtland near Cleveland.

Peter's Reformer Rule: Whenever they smell a rat they want to let the cat out of the bag.

SAMUEL MORSE DAY

ON MAY 24, 1844, Samuel Finley Breese Morse tapped out the message "What Hath God Wrought" in Morse code. It was transmitted on wires between Washington and Baltimore. This inaugurated America's telegraph industry. (The government had appropriated $30,000 for the construction of the line linking Washington to Baltimore.)

The advantage of age is that you can make a fool of yourself in a more dignified manner.

On May 24, 1883, the Brooklyn Bridge, linking the boroughs of Manhattan and Brooklyn in New York City, was opened for the first time to public traffic. The new bridge, designed by John A. Roebling, was the longest suspension bridge in the world to date and consisted of 5,296 galvanized-steel wires bound together.

An income-tax form is like a laundry list—either way you lose your shirt.

Peter's Political-Frustration Principle: The trouble with government is that it scratches when there's no itch.

BABE RUTH FINAL HOME RUN DAY

ON MAY 25, 1935, at Forbes Field, Pittsburgh, Babe Ruth hit his seven hundred and fourteenth—and last—home run. The Babe, always a crowd pleaser, trotted around the bases, doffing his cap to the cheering fans in the stands, thus ending an era in the history of baseball.

If my son is getting as much out of college as the college is getting out of me—he is headed for success.

I never question my wife's judgment—she married me.

Maintain a youthful outlook and in time they'll be calling you a silly old man.

May 25 is African Freedom Day. Member countries of the Organization for African Unity commemorate their independence from colonial rule.

Peter's Natural-Disaster Principle: One touch of nature makes the whole world squirm.

ANDREW JOHNSON ACQUITTAL DAY

May 26

ON MAY 26, 1868, President Andrew Johnson, facing impeachment proceedings in the Senate on charges of "high crimes and misdemeanors," was acquitted by the slim margin of one vote. The leader of the House, Thaddeus Stevens, was so disappointed in the vote that he claimed that henceforth no President could be removed from office by process of law. He predicted, "If tyranny becomes intolerable, the only recourse will be in the dagger of Brutus."

It's better to give than to receive—it's deductible.

The going seems a little easier lately—maybe it's downhill.

One solution to the parking problem is to buy a parked car.

On May 26, 1913, the Actors Equity Association was organized.

Peter's Concern Principle: We should all have some wealth to leave behind—if we want at least a few people sincerely interested in the state of our health.

ON MAY 27, 1818, Amelia Bloomer was born. She was the suffragist remembered for wearing pantaloons which became known as "bloomers."

Nothing makes a little knowledge so dangerous as thinking your spouse doesn't have it.

On May 27, 1957, Senator Theodore F. Green of Rhode Island, at the age of 89 years, 7 months, and 26 days became the oldest man ever to serve in the United States Congress—House or Senate. The record up until that day was held by Representative Charles M. Stedman of North Carolina who died in office in 1930 at the age of 89 years, 7 months, and 25 days.

You're not old if the morning after the night before still makes the night before worth the morning after.

On May 27, 1647, Achsah Young was executed by hanging for being a witch, in the first recorded capital-punishment case of this kind in Massachusetts.

Peter's Safety Rule: Do not drive on a freeway where careless motorists are driving too close ahead of you.

ON MAY 28, 1959, two monkeys named Able and Baker survived a trip into space from Cape Canaveral, Florida. Able and Baker were confined in the nose cone of a rocket and were picked up uninjured.

Early to bed and early to rise—and you're really not one of the regular guys.

Age is catching up with you when, after painting the town red, you need a long rest before applying the second coat.

She didn't seem that good-looking, but at the office party I saw her in a different light—dim.

James Francis Thorpe (Jim Thorpe), American Indian and distinguished athlete, winner of the pentathlon and decathlon in the 1912 Olympic Games, was born May 28, 1888.

Peter's Universal Principle: We cannot solve all the problems of the world at once, but we are capable of messing things up one at a time.

ON MAY 29, 1453, the capital of the Byzantine Empire, Constantinople, was captured by the Turks. Many historians consider this to be the end of the Middle Ages, the beginning of our age.

I painted the town red—after she gave me the brush.

On May 29, 1912, *The New York Sun* reported that 15 young women were dismissed from their jobs at the Curtis Publishing Company in Philadelphia by Edward W. Bok, editor of the *Ladies' Home Journal*, after he observed them dancing the Turkey Trot during their lunch period.

Alimony is where two people make a mistake and one person pays for it.

May 29, 1953, Sir Edmund P. Hillary and Tensing Norkay, a tribesman from Nepal, became the first to reach the summit of Mount Everest.

Peter's Power Principle: Power is nothing more than the capacity to get things done. It is the uses of power that are virtuous or evil.

NORMA CURRIE DAY *May 30*

ON MAY 30, 1978, Norma Currie of Fayetteville, North Carolina, was elected coroner of Cumberland County after promising that if elected she would abolish the office and save the county $41,000.

A hangover is when the dawn comes up like thunder.

May 30 is Memorial Day (also known as Decoration Day). This holiday is a legal observance in those states where it is celebrated. Originally it was intended as a day to honor the memory of those who fell in the War between the States. It is now observed in memory of the nation's dead in all wars.

I was upset when the doctor charged me $200 to tell me I'm going to have to learn to live with it.

On May 30, 1901, the Hall of Fame for Great Americans was dedicated and opened at New York University.

Peter's Validity Principle: The truth of an argument has nothing to do with its credibility.

THE GODIVA PROCESSION, celebrating Lady Godiva's Ride, was first held on May 31, 1678. The original ride came about when Lady Godiva's husband agreed to remit the heavy taxes on the people of Coventry if she would ride naked through the town on a white horse. The Peeping Tom legend, about the man who peeked through closed shutters, was started much later, in the eighteenth century.

My dentist uses a local anesthetic—probably can't afford imported.

On May 31, 1907, a fleet of "taximeter cabs" arrived in New York from Paris. These were the first taxis to be seen in an American city.

Beauty is a skin game.

Walt Whitman, American poet, author of *Leaves of Grass*, was born on May 31, 1819.

Peter's Principle of Age: You're never too old to learn a new area of incompetence.

Modern man tends to believe that competition is the driving force behind progress, but this belief does not stand up to close scrutiny. Competition has no inherent virtue. There is plenty of competition in organized crime. Competition between nations has resulted in development of horrendous weapons. Competition can be the motivating force to produce the best or the worst.

LAURENCE J. PETER,
from *The Peter Plan*

DON'T GIVE UP
THE SHIP DAY

ON JUNE 1, 1813, Captain James Lawrence, commander of the *Chesapeake*, as he was carried mortally wounded from his post on deck during an engagement near Boston with the British frigate *Shannon*, uttered the valiant cry, "Don't give up the ship!" It became part of the language and is used as encouragement to persevere in any kind of trying circumstances.

In the game of love the odds are better for the girl with beauty than the girl with brains because the average male can see better than he can think.

On June 2, 1856, Henry Ward Beecher, a Congregationalist clergyman of Brooklyn, New York, and a vigorous foe of slavery, held a mock public "auction" of a young black girl to expose the evils of slavery.

An adolescent is one who, when not treated like an adult, acts like an infant.

Brigham Young, Mormon Church leader who settled his followers in Salt Lake City, Utah, was born on June 2, 1801.

Peter's Marriage Principle: All marriages are happy—it's living together afterward that can be troublesome.

ON JUNE 2, 1883, 2,000 spectators in Fort Wayne, Indiana, attended the first baseball game to take place at night. Two local teams played at League Park with the aid of 17 floodlights.

Deep breathing increases your longevity—particularly if practiced for 80 to 90 years.

On June 2, 1924, Congress conferred citizenship upon all American Indians.

At commencement they tell the graduates the future is theirs when not even the cap and gown is theirs. There must be a message in the fact that graduation gowns have no pockets.

On June 2, 1835, P. T. Barnum and his circus began their first tour of the United States.

Peter's Medical Prescription: For the person who has everything—antibiotics.

DUKE OF WINDSOR
WEDDING ANNIVERSARY

ON JUNE 3, 1937, the Duke of Windsor, formerly King Edward VIII of Great Britain, was married to Mrs. Wallis Warfield Simpson of Baltimore. He had abdicated the throne on December 11, 1936. The marriage was described by H. L. Mencken as "the greatest news story since the Resurrection."

A problem child is one who puts two and two together and gets curious.

On June 3, 1935, the French liner *Normandie* made her maiden voyage across the Atlantic in 4 days, 11 hours, and 42 seconds, establishing a new record.

Even though children are deductible, they can also be very taxing.

On June 3, 1871, Jesse James, the 24-year-old outlaw robbed the new Obocock Bank in Corydon, Iowa, of $15,000, all the cash in the bank.

Peter's Maxim: There is no rest for the wicked and damn little for the righteous.

JUNE 4 has been observed since 1948 as the day to honor all never-married women who are over 35. This celebration was established by Miss Marian Richards of Norristown, Pennsylvania as a day of fun and humor. Roses and daises are symbols of the day.

A kickback is where things are backwards; the giver says, "Thank you," and the receiver says, "Don't mention it."

On June 4, 1896, Henry Ford moved the first Ford car from a brick shed at 58 Bagley Avenue, Detroit, and drove it around the streets in a successful trial run.

I told the student to go to the end of the line, but he was back in ten seconds complaining that there was someone there already.

On June 4, 1070, a shepherd returned to a cave near Roquefort in France, where he had left an uneaten lunch of bread and goat cheese. The cheese had gone moldy, but tasted delicious. He took some of it to a monastery and soon the monks were curing cheese in the same cave and producing the first Roquefort cheese.

Peter's Medical Theory: The major side effect of medical treatment is bankruptcy.

WORLD ENVIRONMENT DAY   *June 5*

WORLD ENVIRONMENT DAY is observed annually on June 5, the anniversary of the opening of the United Nations Conference on the Human Environment in Stockholm in 1972. The General Assembly has urged marking the day with activities reaffirming concern for preservation and enhancement of the environment.

It might be wiser for the children to take the tranquilizers and the parents the vitamins.

On June 5, 1876, at the Centennial Exposition at Philadelphia, visitors were able to purchase bananas at refreshment stands. Before this bananas had been rarely seen or eaten in the United States.

When it comes to achieving the American Dream you've got to give the American public credit.

On June 5, 1855, the Know Nothing Party, also known as the American Party, held its first national convention in Philadelphia.

Peter's Aging Principle: Old age is all in your head—particularly if you wear dentures, a hearing aid, and bifocals.

ON JUNE 6, 1978, California voters overwhelmingly supported Proposition 13, a primary-election ballot initiative to cut property taxes. This inspired taxpayers in other parts of the country to take similar action.

When it comes to a new product, Americans are aware of the need, Germans create the solution, and the Japanese manufacture it at a price the Americans can afford.

On June 6, 1933, a motion-picture "drive-in" theatre, the first of its kind, was opened in Camden, New Jersey. Space was provided for 500 cars and patrons viewed and heard the film from a screen measuring 40 by 50 feet.

Edward Bellamy, nineteenth-century author of *Looking Backwards*, predicted that in 100 years or so we would not be using cash at all.

On June 6, 1978, Italy's first abortion law took effect. Many Italian doctors became "conscientious objectors."

Peter's Attorney Principle: Any law of over 50 words contains at least one loophole.

BEAU BRUMMELL DAY *June 7*

GEORGE BRYAN BRUMMELL, the man who set the fashion for men's clothes in England, was born on June 7, 1778. As Beau Brummell he was identified with high fashion and his name became synonomous with one who overdresses. The dictionary definition of Beau Brummell is "a dandy or fop."

Do you ever have the uncomfortable feeling that the person you're talking to might be right?

On June 7, 1860, the "dime novel" made its first appearance when a New York publisher issued *Malaeska, the Indian Wife of the White Hunter*, written by Mrs. Ann Stevens. The tale was advertised as "a dollar book for only a dime!"

People who are too scared to steal, too proud to beg, and too poor to pay cash—think credit cards are the answer.

On June 7, 1769, Daniel Boone began his exploration of Kentucky.

Peter's Knowledge-Is-Power Principle: What you don't know won't hurt you, but what you suspect can drive you nuts.

ON JUNE 8, 1869, Ives W. McGaffey of Chicago, Illinois, received a patent for his invention of a machine that revolutionized house cleaning. His device was the vacuum cleaner and was called by the inventor a "sweeping machine."

I believe in Hell, but I also believe in God's mercy, so I am sure that it's empty.

On June 8, 1786, Mr. Hull of 76 Chatham Street, New York, announced in an advertisement in the newspaper that he would start manufacturing ice cream on a commercial basis.

When you go to the dentist, park in a tow-away zone and see how it keeps your mind off the pain.

On June 8, 1978, Naomi James arrived in Dartmouth, completing her solo sail around the world aboard her 53-foot *Express Crusader*.

Peter's Supercompetence Principle: If you're so competent you're irreplaceable you won't be promoted.

MARK TWAIN DAY   *June 9*

ON JUNE 9, 1877, Samuel Langhorne Clemens explained the origin of his pen name in a letter to the editor of the *Daily Alta California*. "Mark Twain was the nom de plume of one Captain Isaiah Sellers, who used to write river news over it for the *New Orleans Picayune*. He died in 1863 and as he could no longer need that signature, I laid violent hands upon it without asking permission of the proprietor's remains. That is the history of the nom de plume I bear. Yours, Samuel L. Clemens."

There would be a lot of contentment in the world if we knew what to remember from the past, what to enjoy in the present, and what to plan for in the future.

On June 9, 1943, after several years of debate, Congress passed an act providing for "pay-as-you-go" income-tax deductions. Employers were authorized to withhold income-tax payments from weekly salary checks of their employees.

Destiny lies ahead!

On June 9, 1965, a Frenchman, Michel Jazy, established a world track record for the mile with a time of 3 minutes, 53.6 seconds.

Peter's Winning Principle: The advantage of seeing both sides of an argument is that it increases your odds of finding how to get around it.

ALCOHOLICS ANONYMOUS FOUNDING DAY

June 10

ON JUNE 10, 1935, in Akron, Ohio, Dr. Robert Smith and William G. Wilson established the Alcoholics Anonymous organization. Alcoholics Anonymous provides a successful program in which alcoholics who have been through AA help other alcoholics who seek assistance.

The pursuit of happiness is guaranteed by the Constitution—but catching it is an individual responsibility.

On June 10, 1776, the Continental Congress appointed a committee to draft a Declaration of Independence. Members of the committee were Thomas Jefferson, Benjamin Franklin, Roger Sherman, John Adams, and Robert R. Livingston.

If happiness could be bought we'd probably be unhappy with the price tag.

On June 10, 1938, Johnny Vander Meer of Cincinnati, Ohio, pitched the first of his successive no-hit baseball games against Boston.

Peter's Timing Principle: The habit of punctuality is the best way of having some time to yourself.

ON JUNE 11, 1963, Governor George Wallace attempted to prevent two black students from registering at the University of Alabama. When confronted by the National Guard he stepped aside and the students registered. This was followed by President John F. Kennedy's address to the nation on racial discrimination: ". . . This nation was founded on the principle that all men are created equal, and the rights of every man are diminished when the rights of one man are threatened . . ."

Find a quiet place for an encounter with yourself.

June 11 is Kamehameha Day, a designated state holiday in Hawaii, honoring the memory of King Kamehameha I who united all the Hawaiian Islands in the eighteenth century.

Inflation is when those who saved for a rainy day really get soaked.

On June 11, 1919, Sir Barton became the first horse to win the Triple Crown of horse racing.

———

Peter's Scientific Principle: Select the right research and you can support any conclusion.

ON JUNE 12, 1922, the first film documentary, *Nanook of the North* by Robert J. Flaherty, was released.

Life is full of questions. For the first 20 years your mother asks, "Where are you going?" For the next 40 years your wife asks, "Where are you going?" And in the end the mourners ask the same question.

On June 12, 1979, the first man-powered flight across the English Channel in the 70-pound *Gossamer Albatross* took 2 hours and 49 minutes.

Politics is very simple: anything bad during an administration they inherited—anything good, they created.

On June 12, 1923, in New York, Harry Houdini, the magician, escaped from a straitjacket while suspended head downward forty feet above the large, cheering audience on the ground.

Peter's Stress Principle: You can get run-down by being too wound up.

ON JUNE 13, 1927, millions of New Yorkers turned out to welcome Charles A. Lindbergh after he flew to their city from Washington accompanied by an Army air escort of 23 planes. During the parade in his honor, 750,000 pounds of paper and ticker tape were showered on the aviator and his entourage. At City Hall, Mayor James J. Walker said, "You can hear the heartbeat of the six million people that live in this City. . . . New York City is yours—I don't give it to you—you won it."

Why do so many complain that they can't remember and so few that they can't think?

On June 13, 1789, Mrs. Alexander Hamilton gave a dinner party for General George Washington and surprised and delighted her guests by serving ice cream for dessert.

Today it is hard to believe that this country was founded as a protest against taxation.

On June 13, 1967, President Johnson nominated Thurgood Marshall to the Supreme Court, making him the first black to become a Supreme Court Justice.

Peter's Parental Principle: One advantage of raising a family to getting rich is that you're willing to admit when you've had enough.

FLAG DAY   *June 14*

A PRESIDENTIAL PROCLAMATION issued in 1916 and covering all succeeding years makes June 14 Flag Day. On June 14, 1777, John Adams introduced a resolution before the Continental Congress making thirteen red and white stripes and thirteen stars the flag of the thirteen colonies.

Corrupt politicians, thrown out of office, write books about their experience—it's a case of perish and publish.

On June 14, 1953, President Dwight D. Eisenhower, speaking at Dartmouth College, assailed "book burners," saying: "Don't join the book burners. Don't think you are going to conceal thoughts by concealing evidence that they ever existed. . . . How will we defeat communism unless we know what it is and why it has such an appeal for men?"

The best test of a sense of humor is to tell a person that he doesn't have one.

On June 14, 1846, California was established as a republic independent of Mexico.

Peter's Systems Theory: Free enterprise is the worst possible system, but we put up with it because all the others are worse.

ON JUNE 15, 1752, Benjamin Franklin flew a kite during a lightning storm to prove that lightning was a discharge of electricity.

Absence makes the heart grow fonder—but presents work well too.

June 15 is also Smile Power Day, to remind us that a smile creates a happier life and a better world.

One of my creditors called and said, "We've done more for you than your own mother. She only carried you for nine months and we've carried you for a year."

On June 15, 1215, at Runnymede, England, King John was forced to sign the Magna Carta, the basic document of Anglo-Saxon law.

Peter's Democratic Principle: The right to be wrong is not the right to do wrong.

ON JUNE 16, 1964, Mrs. Endicott Peabody, wife of the governor of Massachusetts, was guest of honor at a unique social event. At a tea party given by the cleaning women of the State House in Boston, a spokeswoman for the scrubwomen presented the governor's wife with a plaque which read, "For her gracious and kind understanding of the problems of others. . . . She is our proven friend."

The accent may be on youth, but the stress is on parents.

On June 16, 1963, Valentina Tereshkova became the First Woman in Space when she manually controlled the USSR *Vostok VI* for 48 orbits in space.

She wasn't much of a mathematician, but she put two and two together and got my number.

On June 16, 1858, Abraham Lincoln uttered the now famous words, "A house divided against itself cannot stand."

Peter's Digestive Theory: It's a strong stomach that has no turning.

GI JOE DAY   *June 17*

ON JUNE 17, 1942, the term GI Joe appeared for the first time in Lieutenant Dave Berger's comic strip in the army weekly magazine *Yank* during World War II.

Everybody should do as he likes even if he has to be forced to do so.

June 17 is Watergate Day, the anniversary of the arrests at the Democratic party headquarters leading to revelations of political espionage. As a result President Richard M. Nixon resigned.

Time wounds all heels.

On June 17, 1947, Pan American Airways started the first round-the-world airline service from New York.

Peter's Discretion Principle: If you're old enough to know better, you're too old to do it.

INTERNATIONAL PICNIC DAY   *June 18*

JUNE 18 is identified as the day to celebrate that great international summer event, the picnic.

Money can't buy happiness, but it supports the kind of misery you can handle.

On June 18, 1812, the Congress declared war on England, and for the second time in American history, the United States was at war with Great Britain.

What this country needs is a spot remover to remove those spots left by spot removers.

On June 18, 1898, a critic in *The New York Times* said that George Bernard Shaw's literary career showed no promise. He wrote, "This voluble jack-of-all-trades, this so-called Socialist, this vociferous advocate of plain fare and industrial reform . . . who devotes all his time to word-juggling about the arts of music and drama . . . this carnivorous vegetarian cannot be judged by his own standards when he puts his wares on the open market."

Peter's Literary Principle: Some writing is not as dull as some of its readers.

THE FIRST OBSERVANCE OF FATHER'S DAY took place on June 19, 1910, in Spokane, Washington. The idea for the day was sponsored by Mrs. John Bruce Dodd. Jane Addams wrote, "Poor father has been left out in the cold. He doesn't get much recognition. But regardless of his breadwinning proclivities, it would be a good thing if he had a day that would mean recognition for him." Father's Day is now observed on the third Sunday of June.

Advice is like mushrooms—accepting the wrong kind can be fatal.

On June 19, 1912, the United States government adopted the eight-hour day for all its employees.

Psychological adjustment is watching an old late-night movie—*Remember Pearl Harbor*—on a Sony.

On June 19, 1855, the Statue of Liberty arrived at Bedloe's Island in New York Harbor.

Peter's Hypocritical Principle: We are nicer to an unpleasant celebrity than we are to someone who is just unpleasant.

LIZZIE BORDEN
ACQUITTAL DAY

ON JUNE 20, 1893, in New Bedford, Massachusetts, Lizzie Borden was acquitted of the murder of her father and step-mother in a sensational case. On August 4, 1892, her parents had been found hacked to death in the family home. The much publicized murder inspired the jingle:

> Lizzie Borden took an ax
> And gave her mother forty whacks.
> When she saw what she had done
> She gave her father forty-one.

In 25 years these will be the good old days.

On June 20, 1910, Fanny Brice made her debut in the Ziegfeld Follies, and critics and public alike recognized a great new comedy star.

How can you respect morticians? All they want is your body.

On June 20, 1782, "E Pluribus Unum," the legend on the Great Seal of the United States, was adopted by Congress.

Peter's Accountability-in-Education Principle: No athlete should be awarded a letter unless he can read it.

ON JUNE 21, 1788, New Hampshire became the ninth state to ratify the Constitution, thereby causing it to go into effect. The last article of the Constitution reads: "The Ratification of the Conventions of nine States shall be sufficient for the Establishment of this Constitution between the States so ratifying the Same."

Sometimes, silence is golden—sometimes, it's a yellow streak.

On June 21, 1954, the American Cancer Society reported that "heavy" cigarette smokers, aged 50 to 70, have a death rate up to 75 percent higher than nonsmokers.

If at first you don't succeed—don't play Russian roulette.

On June 21, 1948, Dr. Peter Goldmark of the CBS Laboratories demonstrated a new invention, the long-playing phonograph record.

Peter's Law of Philosophical Appreciation: Anticipating applause for a profound intellectual contribution is as futile as dropping a feather down a well and waiting for the splash.

On June 22, 1910, Count Zeppelin started the first airship passenger service between Friedrichshafen and Düsseldorf, a distance of 300 miles. The first airship was called the *Deutschland*.

You're a grown-up when you stop belonging to the younger generation and start complaining about it.

On this day in 1941, Hitler's forces attacked the USSR.

We give little thought to our destinations as long as we can outdistance our pursuers.

On June 22, 1970, President Nixon signed into law a bill giving eighteen-year-olds the right to vote.

Peter's Law of the West: If you shoot first and ask questions after, you are not going to get many answers.

ON JUNE 23, 1868, a Wisconsin journalist and state senator, Christopher Latham Sholes, received a patent for his "Type Writer." THE MACHINE HAD CAPITAL LETTERS ONLY.

How can we stop adultery when we can't even make it unpopular?

The Secret Service was created by an Act of Congress on June 23, 1860.

He took her to a retreat in order to make advances.

On June 23, 1961, an international treaty was signed for scientific cooperation and the peaceful use of the Antarctic.

Peter's Differential Principle: In a dictatorship the people are afraid to tell the truth to the leaders, and in a democracy the leaders are afraid to tell the truth to the people.

ON JUNE 24, 1647, Margaret Brent, a niece of Lord Baltimore, appeared before the Maryland Assembly and demanded both a voice and a vote for herself in that assembly. The all-male body was completely shocked by Mistress Brent, the first suffragette in America.

A pipe gives a wise man time to think and a fool something to stick in his mouth.

On June 24, 1942, the Royal Family of the Netherlands, in exile since the Nazi occupation of their homeland, arrived in the United States to establish temporary residence here.

Bankruptcy is the kiss of debt.

On June 24, 1947, the first reported sightings of flying saucers came from the area of Mount Rainer, Washington. Kenneth Arnold of Boise, Idaho, claimed he observed nine "saucer-like objects" flying in formation.

Peter's Detection Principle: Things are lost only when you're looking where they aren't.

COLOR TELEVISION DAY *June 25*

ON JUNE 25, 1951, the Columbia Broadcasting System presented the first commercial color-television program in history. Broadcast from New York City, the hour-long show featured, among others, Arthur Godfrey, Faye Emerson, Sam Levenson, and Ed Sullivan.

A penny saved is a penny taxed.

On June 25, 1874, Rose Cecil O'Neill, the illustrator who first drew the plump cupids that were later patented as Kewpie dolls, was born.

On June 25, 1630, Governor John Winthrop introduced the table fork to America.

On June 25, 1876, General George Custer went down to defeat in the battle called "Custer's Last Stand," at Little Big Horn, Montana.

Peter's Campaign Principle: While the people try to find what the candidate stands for, the candidate tries to find what the people will stand for.

ON JUNE 26, 1959, President Eisenhower and Queen Elizabeth II jointly officiated at the opening and dedication of the St. Lawrence Seaway, at St. Lambert, Quebec.

Yesterday children asked you where they came from—today they tell you where to go.

We will become an endangered species not because we have loved too much but because we have loved too little.

On June 26, 1870, in Atlantic City, New Jersey, the world's first boardwalk was completed.

On June 26, 1945, the Charter of the United Nations was signed in San Francisco, California.

Peter's Pleasure Principle: Joy can't be preserved for future use, so you've got to make it fresh every day.

ON JUNE 27, 1923, Captain Lowell Smith, while flying over Coronado, California, lowered a 40-foot steel-wire-encased hose from his De Havilland plane and fueled the plane piloted by Lieutenant Richter in the first successful midair refueling.

We develop subdivisions by cutting down all the trees and then naming the streets after them.

On April 7, 1787, the English historian Edward Gibbon completed the writing of his monumental work, *The Decline and Fall of the Roman Empire.*

Nature punishes for most sins, but dishonesty, theft, and libel are not in her jurisdiction—we must take action against them.

On June 27, 1936, Franklin D. Roosevelt spoke these now famous words: "This generation of Americans has a rendezvous with destiny."

Peter's Bureaucratic-Cost Principle: The cost of any action increases in direct ratio to the number of approvals required to take that action.

IN RESPONSE TO REQUESTS that he become a presidential candidate, Will Rogers in his column of June 28, 1931, wrote: "I not only 'don't choose to run' but I don't want to leave a loophole in case I am drafted, so I won't choose. I will say 'won't run' no matter how bad the country will need a comedian by that time."

An ideal husband is one who thinks his wife's headache is as important as his own ulcer.

On June 28, 1914, a young Serbian fanatic, Gavrilo Princip, assassinated the heir to the Austro-Hungarian throne, Archduke Francis Ferdinand, and his wife. This incident started World War I.

I would rather be able to appreciate things I cannot have than to have things I cannot appreciate.

On June 28, 1886, William E. Gladstone said, "All the world over, I will back the masses against the classes."

Peter's Junk-Mail Principle: The postman bringeth and the trashman taketh away.

FEAST OF SAINT PETER AND SAINT PAUL

THE FEAST OF Saint Peter and Saint Paul has been celebrated on June 29 since early in the Christian era. By the end of the fourth century great crowds flocked to Rome annually for the feast, making a pilgrimage from St. Peter's Basilica to St. Paul's on the other side of the city. Both Peter and Paul had been devout Jews, but became the two strongest pillars of the infant Christian Church. Great powers have been attributed to them in the past, but less fancifully, Saint Paul is the patron saint of tentmakers, theologians, and ropemakers, and Saint Peter is the patron saint of fishermen and sailors.

If it's difficult to dust, it's probably an antique.

On June 29, 1954, the writer Quentin Reynolds was awarded damages against columnist Westbrook Pegler in a bitterly fought libel trial.

A curious illusion besets mankind that we are normally and mentally superior to those who differ from us in belief.

On June 29, 1785, Miss L. Sage became the first Englishwoman to fly in a balloon. She flew from London to Middlesex in three hours.

Peter's Fatalistic Principle: It is better to stand in the doorway and wait for the storm to pass than to depend on someone who promises to part the clouds.

BRODIN'S CONQUEST OF NIAGARA FALLS DAY

ON JUNE 30, 1859, a French acrobat and aerialist, Charles Brodin, walked across Niagara Falls on a tightrope. The walk, requiring only about five minutes, was witnessed by a crowd of over 25,000 persons. Brodin, whose real name was Jean Francois Gravelet, later followed this feat with crossing while (1) blindfolded, (2) pushing a wheelbarrow, (3) carrying a man on his back, and (4) walking on stilts.

There are two sides to every political issue—the problem is after you listen to both sides, you haven't heard much.

On April 30, 1899, Charles M. (Mile-a-Minute) Murphy rode a bicycle for a mile in 57 ⅘ seconds, paced by a special railway car.

If we can become loving and kind, not merely respectable, the problem will be solved.

On June 30, 1852, Henry David Thoreau wrote, "A lover of Nature is a lover of man. If I have no friend, what is Nature to me."

Peter's Principle of Technological Progress: I used to turn the TV off—now it turns me off.

July

DOMINION DAY IN CANADA

JULY 1 IS A NATIONAL holiday in Canada, celebrating the confederation of Canadian provinces into the Dominion of Canada on this day in 1867, under the British North American Act.

I'm sure grateful for daylight saving—my garden needs the extra hour of sunlight.

July 1, 1940, was the completion day for the Tacoma Narrows Bridge.

The repairman won't fix my air-conditioner—claims it's too hot in my apartment.

On July 1, 1948, the five-cent subway fare was ended in New York City.

Peter's Creativity Principle: All mental effort not directed toward solving a substantive problem is directed toward mischief.

DECLARATION OF INDEPENDENCE RESOLUTION

THE ADOPTION OF a resolution by the Continental Congress in Philadelphia, July 2, 1776, paved the way for adoption on July 4, 1776, of the Declaration of Independence. This resolution stated: "Resolved, That these United Colonies are, and of right ought to be, free and independent States, that they are absolved from all allegiance to the British Crown, and that all political connection between them and the State of Great Britain is, and ought to be, totally dissolved. That it is expedient forthwith to take the most effectual measures for forming foreign Alliances. That a plan of confederation be prepared and transmitted to the respective Colonies for their consideration and approbation."

Today's bathing suits are really something—if you can call nothing something.

My wife does a bird imitation—she watches me like a hawk.

Our new air-conditioner has an automatic feature—every time the weather gets very hot it automatically breaks down.

On July 2, 1964, President Johnson signed the Civil Rights Act.

Peter's Ingenuity Principle: An unbreakable toy can always be used to break other toys.

ON JULY 3, 303, in Rome, executioners were dispatched with orders to kill a man called Phocas. Unknown to them they stopped at Phocas's house for refreshments. Phocas received them with his usual hospitality. When he learned of their mission, he told the executioners that he was the man for whom they were searching. After recovering from their surprise, they cut off his head.

I had a problem—where do you complain about the complaint department?

Stopping research to save money is like stopping your watch to save time.

The secret of health is to eat garlic every day—the problem is that it isn't a secret for long.

On July 3, 1819, the first savings bank in America opened its doors to the public. The Bank of Savings in New York City had 80 depositors on the first day, depositing a total of $2,807.

Peter's Jealous Principle: The bigger they are, the harder others try to make them fall.

INDEPENDENCE DAY   *July 4*

THIS LEGAL HOLIDAY in the United States and its territories commemorates adoption by the Continental Congress of the Declaration of Independence, July 4, 1776.

July 4 is devoted to shooting things off—firecrackers, skyrockets, and mouths.

July 4 is also the occasion for two special athletic events: the "International Cherry Pit Spitting Contest," held at Eau Claire, Michigan, and the "Stone Skipping Open Tournament," held at Mackinac Island, Michigan.

It was most considerate of the founding fathers to sign the Declaration of Independence on a holiday.

On July 4, 1918, Woodrow Wilson said, "What we seek is the reign of law, based upon the consent of the governed and sustained by the organized opinion of mankind."

Peter's Credit Principle: Staying out of debt may be a good idea, but people will think you're a poor credit risk.

ON JULY 5, 1865, William Booth founded the Salvation Army in London, England.

Every American still has a chance to become President—that's one of the risks he has to take.

On July 5, 1942, Edsel Ford, whose family has manufactured 30 million automobiles since 1903, could not get a new car for his own use until a World War II rationing board considered his application.

Maybe George Washington never told a lie—but in those days no one had to fill out an income-tax form.

On July 5, 1935, the National Labor Relations Board was authorized by the presidential signature of the Wagner-Connery Act.

Peter's Input-Output Principle: Things just don't add up—our garbage weighs more than our groceries.

TALKING PICTURE DAY *July 6*

THE PREVIEW OF THE FIRST all-talking motion picture, *Lights of New York*, took place at New York's Strand Theatre on July 6, 1928.

Age doesn't really matter—unless you're a cheese.

On July 6, 1885, Louis Pasteur inoculated the first human being, a boy who had been bitten by a rabid dog. The boy, Joseph Meister, did not develop the disease and later became superintendent of the Pasteur Institute.

It is very annoying to have some bore go right on talking when you are interrupting.

On July 6, 1933, the first all-star National versus American League baseball game took place in Chicago. The American League won 5-2.

Peter's Stress-Avoidance Principle: Hard work will not hurt you—as long as you never get too close to it.

ON JULY 7, 1946, Mother Francis Xavier Cabrini was canonized by Pope Pius XII, thus becoming the first United States citizen to be made a saint.

Why am I fond of people who agree with me and food that doesn't?

On July 7, 1865, four persons named as accomplices of John Wilkes Booth in the assassination of Abraham Lincoln were hanged. They were Mrs. Mary E. Surratt, David E. Herold, George A. Atzerodt, and Lewis Payne.

If we lacked imagination enough to foresee something better, life would indeed be a tragedy.

On July 7, 1898, United States annexation of the Hawaiian Islands was authorized, with the formal transfer of sovereignty on August 12.

Peter's Horse-and-Buggy Principle: A good thing about the horse-and-buggy days is that we didn't have to make deals with Eastern countries to get oats.

FIRST UNITED STATES PASSPORT DAY

ON JULY 8, 1796, Francis Barre, being "a citizen having occasion to pass into foreign countries about his lawful affairs," was granted a passport, the first to be issued, by the Passport Division of the U.S. State Department.

Modern air travel is making the earth smaller, but you still can't fall and miss it.

On July 8, 1947, Laurence Olivier was knighted, becoming the youngest actor to be so honored.

A miracle is an event described by those to whom it was told by those who did not see it.

On July 8, 1915, H. G. Wells wrote to Henry James: "To you literature like painting is an end, to me literature like architecture is a means, it has a use."

Peter's First Principles: (1) A martyr is a hero who didn't make it. (2) Martyrs set bad examples. (3) Some days it is better to stay in bed.

GOAT MOTHER DAY

ON JULY 9, 1812, the British frigate *Swallow* engaged in battle with a French vessel near Majorca. One of the English sailors, Phelan by name, had his wife and infant son, Tommy, on board. The parents were both killed and buried at sea. Tommy, who was only three weeks old, was placed with a female Maltese goat that belonged to the captain. The goat became accustomed to the child and would lie down voluntarily to suckle him. The goat was a successful surrogate mother, and Tommy grew and prospered and became a sailor.

I've just invented an alarm clock you can set on Saturday night to ring on Monday morning.

On July 9, 1945, Mayor Fiorello La Guardia, during a newspaper strike in New York, read the comic strips, provided by the cartoonists, over radio station WNYC.

He only drinks to fill in the time until he is drunk.

On July 9, 1763, Samuel Johnson said, "A man ought to read just as inclination leads him; for what he reads as a task will do him no good."

Peter's Modern-Transportation Principle: There is no longer any such thing as a distant relative.

UNITED STATES
HOTTEST DAY

ON JULY 10, 1913, in Death Valley, California, the thermometer hit 134°F., the highest temperature ever recorded in the United States.

Success is the realization of the estimate you placed upon yourself.

On July 10, 1958, Robert Earl Hughes was buried in Benville Cemetery, Illinois. His weight was 1,069 pounds, the highest weight ever for human remains.

Genius is the ability to act wisely without precedent—to do the right thing for the first time.

On July 10, 1958, after 13 years in a mental hospital in Washington, D.C., Ezra Pound returned to Italy and told reporters, "All America is an insane asylum."

Peter's Hierarchial Principle: Most jobs are like being one of a sled-dog team—nobody gets a change of scene except the lead dog.

NATIONAL CHEER UP THE LONELY DAY

July 11

THIS DAY IS DEDICATED to help stamp out loneliness by becoming a Cheerer Upper and visiting shut-ins and the lonely in hospitals and nursing homes.

Our lives are all interrelated—self-reliance is essential, but there is no such thing as independence.

On July 11, 1944, President Franklin D. Roosevelt, the only Chief Executive to be elected to a third term of office, announced he was available for a fourth term, saying, "If the Convention should nominate me, I shall accept. If the people elect me, I will serve."

The Civil War was a draw—the North won it in the history books and the South won it in the novels.

On July 11, 1936, the Triborough Bridge was opened, linking Manhattan, the Bronx, and Queens.

Peter's Interesting Theory: Even boredom can be interesting if you become involved in exploring the causes of boredom.

JULY 12 IS THE DAY of annual observance commemorating the
Battle of Boyne in 1690. The forces of King William III of England,
Prince of Orange, defeated the forces of James II at Boyne River
in Ireland. In Northern Ireland the Battle of Boyne is celebrated
as a National Holiday.

We dream of the wonders of a carefree life on an island where
people were not so bothered, but why not consider the earth an
island and perform our wonders here and now?

On July 12, 1810, members of the Journeymen Cordwainers, a
shoemakers' union, went on trial in New York City for having
called a strike to win a wage increase. The court found the union
guilty and fined each member a dollar plus legal costs.

All that glitters is not brass.

On July 12, 1933, the United States established the minimum
wage of 40 cents an hour.

Peter's Policy Principle: Honesty is the best policy—there is less
competition.

ON JULY 13, 1865, in an editorial in *The New York Tribune*, Horace Greeley gave advice to federal civil servants, who were complaining about high living costs and low salaries in the national capital. "Washington is not a place to live in. The rents are high, the food is bad, the dust is disgusting and the morals are deplorable. Go west, young man, go west." Many followed his advice. "Go west, young man" became popular all over the country. Mr. Greeley later admitted he borrowed the phrase from the *Terre Haute Express* in Indiana.

Power manifests itself in conspicuous waste—until conspicuous waste imagines itself power.

You can't fool all of the people all of the time—but that really isn't necessary.

An alcoholic is anyone who will drink with anyone to anyone.

On July 13, 1925, Will Rogers became a temporary replacement for W. C. Fields in the Zeigfeld Follies, when Fields was on leave because of the death of his mother. Rogers, with no advance notice, was a great success.

Peter's Expectation Principle: When campaigning, politicians promise us a more abundant life, but when elected they tell us to lower our expectations.

BASTILLE DAY *July 14*

THIS FRENCH NATIONAL HOLIDAY is observed in commemoration of the storming of the Bastille prison by the citizens of Paris on July 14, 1789, and the release of all the monarchy's political prisoners. The Bastille consisted of eight stone towers surrounded by a moat 120 yards wide. Its dungeons and cages were infamous and had long been a symbol of despotic royal power. On July 14, 1943, *The New York Times* commented, "Bastille Day is the holiday for all free men. It is a day given us in trust by the people of France, against the day of their liberation, the restoration of the rights of man."

A picture may be worth a thousand words—but not when you're on the phone.

An eccentric is one who keeps within his budget, carries no snapshots of his children, and drives more slowly than the speed limit.

The way he brags about his ancestors you'd think he had selected them himself.

On July 14, 1881, Billy the Kid was killed by Sheriff Pat Garrett at Fort Sumner, New Mexico.

Peter's Simplistic Principle: All difficult problems have easy, simple, understandable, wrong solutions.

SAINT SWITHIN, born in Hampshire, England in A.D. 800, became Bishop of Winchester and Royal Counselor to King Egbert and King Aethelwulf. According to his wishes, upon his death in 862 he was buried outside Winchester Cathedral where "he would be exposed to the feet of passersby and the drops falling from above." July 15, 971 was declared Saint Swithin's Feast Day and on that day his remains were transferred from the yard to the cathedral. He sent rain that lasted for 40 days. This miracle performed 109 years after his death precipitated the spread of Saint Swithin's cult and established the old meteorological superstition:

> St. Swithin's day if thou dost rain,
> For forty days it will remain;
> St. Swithin's day if thou be fair,
> For forty days 'twill rain nae mair.

My ambition was to marry a rich woman who was too proud to have her husband work.

On July 15, 1876, George Washington Bradley pitched the first no-hit baseball game in history, while playing for St. Louis against Hartford. Score 2–0.

An economist is an expert who will know tomorrow why the things he predicted yesterday didn't happen today.

July 15 is National Ice Cream Day to honor dairy farmers and ice-cream makers.

Peter's Agency-Accessibility Principle: The door to bureaucracy is locked from the inside.

ON JULY 16, 1969, astronauts Neil Armstrong, Edwin Aldrin, Jr., and Michael Collins blasted off in spaceship *Apollo II* from Cape Kennedy, Florida, on the first voyage to land on the moon, arriving July 20.

About the only advantage of growing old is that you will never have to do it over again.

On July 16, 1790, Congress established the District of Columbia on the Potomac River, voting to set up there the permanent seat of the government of the United States.

An editor is one who separates the wheat from the chaff and then prints the chaff.

On July 16, 1964, Barry M. Goldwater said, "I would remind you that extremism in the defense of liberty is no vice. And let me remind you also that moderation in the pursuit of justice is no virtue."

Peter's Creativity Law: The way to inspire new thoughts is to seal the letter.

WRONG WAY CORRIGAN DAY   *July 17*

ON JULY 17, 1938, Douglas Corrigan took off, intending to fly from New York to California but landing his plane in Dublin, Ireland, the next day. Americans immediately gave him the nickname, "Wrong Way Corrigan."

Speak when you're angry—and you'll make the best speech you'll ever regret.

On July 17, 1955, Arco, Idaho, a town of 1,350 persons, became the first community in the world to receive all its power from atomic energy. For one hour, electricity from an experimental nuclear plant some 20 miles away was transmitted to all users over conventional power lines.

The universal form of compulsory education is experience.

On July 17, 1955, an American institution, Disneyland, opened in Anaheim, California.

Peter's MPG Quandary: Why should any energy shortage matter when the country is running downhill?

ANTIBIGOT DAY

THE ANTIBIGOT CELEBRATION is sponsored by the Tolerants to spoof bigoted claims to infallibility and omniscience. Nonbigots tolerantly accept the existence of many right ways to live.

If you really want to know where he stands, see him when he's beside himself.

On July 18, 1872, at a "grand scientific soirée" held in Albert Hall, London, England, a telegraphic experiment was made in which messages were interchanged between Albert Hall and Teheran as well as with an Indian state.

Antique chairs are uncomfortable because the comfortable ones were worn out years ago.

July 18 is Rome Burns Twice Day. On July 18, 390 B.C., Rome was burned and sacked by Brennus of Gaul. On July 18, A.D. 64, Rome burned again while Nero fiddled.

Peter's Photographic Law: The best shots occur immediately after all the film is used up.

ON JULY 19, 1848, in Seneca Falls, New Jersey, the first women's rights convention in America adopted the Declaration of Sentiments and Resolutions that inaugurated the women's suffrage movement.

Knitting is a good hobby—it gives you something to think about while watching television.

An efficiency expert is a trained person who believes in economy at any cost.

On July 19, 1692, in Massachusetts, a woman of blameless life, Rebecca Nurse, was taken to church in chains, excommunicated as a witch, and hanged.

On July 19, 1842, at a trotting race in Hoxton, England, a gray pony ridden by a monkey dressed in a racing costume completed the race, a distance of 4 miles, in 57 minutes.

Peter's Theory of Urban Decay: Nobody goes downtown anymore because it's too crowded.

ON JULY 20, 1969, two United States astronauts, Neil Armstrong and Edwin Aldrin, Jr., landed the lunar module *Eagle* on the surface of the moon where it remained for 21 hours, 36 minutes, 16 seconds. Aldrin and Armstrong walked on the moon for approximately 2¼ hours.

If I am wrong, I'm willing to be forgiven.

On July 20, 1859, baseball fans were charged an admission fee for the first time. To see Brooklyn play New York 1,500 spectators paid 50 cents each.

The thing I like about egotists is that they don't go around talking about other people.

On July 20, 1969, Neil Armstrong, the first man to set foot on the moon, said, "That's one small step for man, one giant leap for mankind."

Peter's Historical Principle: We do not learn very much from history, and that's the most important lesson that history teaches us.

ON JULY 21, 1828, at Paterson, New Jersey, for the first time the militia was called in to control strikers. The workers were protesting the movement of the factory dinner hour from noon to one o'clock. They claimed that they were too hungry by one. The earlier midday break had caused the name "dinner pail" to be changed to "lunch pail."

Appearances are deceiving, but disappearances are even more so.

On July 21, 1873, Jesse James committed the world's first train robbery at Adair, Iowa, and escaped with $3,000.

After every election the American way is to unite behind the new administration—and blame it for everything.

On July 21, 1978, the National Women's Hall of Fame was dedicated, honoring the American women whose contributions to the development of their country have been the greatest.

Peter's Efficiency Rule: Avoid duplication. I repeat, avoid duplication.

SPOONER'S DAY

THIS DAY IS NAMED in memory of the Reverend William Archibald Spooner, Warden of New College, Oxford, England. He was born in London on July 22, 1844. His frequent slips of the tongue led to the term "spoonerism." His accidental transpositions gave us "blushing crow" (for crushing blow), "tons of soil" (for sons of toil), "queer old dear" (for dear old queer), "swell foop" (for fell swoop), and many others.

Archaeologists spend their time digging in the earth in an attempt to find a civilization worse than ours.

On this day in 1920, Warren G. Harding said "We must stabilize and strive for normalcy."

An election is the one race in which most people pick the winner.

On July 22, 1849, Emma Lazarus was born. Her poem "Give me your tired, your poor . . ." is inscribed on the Statue of Liberty.

Peter's Gastronomy Principle: No matter how little you expect from a TV dinner, you will be disappointed.

ON JULY 23, 1904, the ice-cream cone was born when Charles E. Minches of St. Louis, Missouri, called on a young lady, carrying in one hand a bouquet of flowers and in the other an ice-cream sandwich. Looking for a vase for the flowers, the young lady fashioned one out of the sandwich wafer, thereby suggesting to her caller a way of serving a scoop of ice cream.

There are two types of people—those who divide people into two types and those who do not.

On July 23, 1886, Steve Brodie claimed he had jumped off the Brooklyn Bridge earlier that day. He did it for publicity, and as a result attention-seeking exploits became known as "pulling a brodie."

An election is a conflict of interests diagnosed as a contest of principles.

On July 23, 1846, Henry David Thoreau was sent to jail for refusing to pay his poll tax. The experience inspired him to write "Civil Disobedience."

Peter's Gastronomic Law: Indigestion results when an optimistic appetite confronts a pessimistic digestion.

THIS IS THE PLACE ANNIVERSARY

ON JULY 24, 1847, Brigham Young, leading a party of Mormon pioneers, reached the present site of Salt Lake City. Young, who was riding in a carriage, was driven to a height from which he could see the surrounding country. When he saw the splendid panorama of the valley in Utah spread out below he said, "This is the place." This phrase became associated with Salt Lake City and the famous statue of Brigham Young with outstretched arm is called the This Is The Place Statue.

Life is a party at which you arrive after it has started, and leave before it has ended.

On the day in 1915, the excursion boat *Eastland* capsized in the Chicago River.

Art is a paradox—if you want to master it, you must become its slave.

Amelia Earhart, the first woman to fly solo across the Atlantic and the Pacific, from Hawaii to California, was born on July 24, 1897.

Peter's Sermon on the Mount: The mountain will be there whether you climb it or not.

ON JULY 25, 1978, Louise Brown, 5 pounds, 12 ounces, was born at Oldham, England. Hers was the first documented birth of a baby conceived outside the body of a woman. The parents were Gilbert John and Lesley Brown. The physicians were Patrick Christopher Steptoe and R. Geoffrey Edwards.

What is going to replace automation?

On July 25, 1956, the ships *Stockholm* and *Andrea Doria* collided.

I have trouble getting into a car that's more compact than I am.

On July 25, 1909, Louis Blériot made the first airplane flight across the English Channel from Calais, France, to Dover, England.

Peter's First Amendment: I don't approve of the message on your T-shirt, but I'll defend your right to wear it.

JOHN WILMOT WAS the Earl of Rochester and leader of the court surrounding King Charles II. He led His Majesty in many wild pranks and assorted debaucheries. His wit was at its best toward the end of each drinking bout so the king saw to it that he was seldom sober. He wrote satirical poems about anyone including King Charles II. He once wrote a mock epitaph on the king's bedchamber door.

> Here lies our sovereign lord and king,
> Whose word no man relies on;
> Who never says a foolish thing;
> Nor ever does a wise one.

The poetry and carousing ended with his death on July 26, 1860.

Tact is the art of putting your foot down without stepping on anyone's toes.

Children brighten up a home—because they leave the lights on all over the house.

The delight of creative work lies in self-discovery—each find is a glad surprise.

On July 26, 1963, President John F. Kennedy addressed the nation on the nuclear-test-ban treaty: "This treaty is not the millennium. It will not resolve all conflicts, or cause the Communists to forgo their ambitions, or eliminate the dangers of war. . . . but it is an important first step—a step toward reason—a step away from war."

Peter's Axiomatic Principle: No matter where you go, that's where you'll be.

On July 27, 1866, the Atlantic cable laying was successfully completed. After 12 years of remarkable faith and toil, Cyrus W. Field succeeded in laying a reliable working cable, 1,686 miles long, between the New World in Newfoundland and the old at Valentia on the Irish coast. Four previous attempts had failed.

Take your choice: talk about others and be a gossip or talk about yourself and be a bore.

We could reduce arguments if we tried to determine what's right instead of who's right.

The boss said, "We have a special incentive plan—we fire you at the drop of a hat."

On her deathbed, July 27, 1946, Gertrude Stein uttered her last words when she asked Alice B. Toklas, "What is the answer?" After a pause and no answer, she asked, "In that case what is the question?"

Peter's Forecasting Principle: The best system for predicting the future is called pessimism.

SINGING TELEGRAM DAY July 28

ON JULY 28, 1933, the first singing telegram is said to have been delivered to singer Rudy Vallee on his thirty-second birthday. Early singing telegrams were delivered in person by a uniformed messenger traveling on a bicycle. More recently, singing telegrams have been delivered by telephone.

An autobiography is a work of literature based on the art of self-defense.

On July 28, 1932, more than 15,000 unemployed war veterans camped in Washington demanding payment of "war bonuses." They were driven out by federal troops commanded by General Douglas MacArthur.

A typical tourist wants to go to places where there are no tourists.

Anne Hutchinson, born on July 28, 1591, was banished from Boston for saying women should have a voice in church affairs.

Peter's Postulate: Superman is never around when you need him.

PRESIDENT RATING DAY

ON JULY 29, 1962, a poll among 75 noted American historians rated the presidents of the United States in five categories: (1) Great: Lincoln, Washington, Franklin D. Roosevelt, Wilson, and Jefferson, (2) Near Great: Jackson, Theodore Roosevelt, Polk, Truman, John Adams, and Cleveland; (3) Average: Madison, John Quincy Adams, Hayes, McKinley, Taft, Van Buren, Monroe, Hoover, Benjamin Harrison, Arthur, Eisenhower, and Andrew Johnson; (4) Below Average: Taylor, Tyler, Filmore, Coolidge, Pierce, Buchanan; (5) Failure: Grant and Harding.

A short person looking up sees farther than a tall person looking down.

On July 29, 1914, the first United States transcontinental telephone conversation took place between New York and San Francisco.

Everyone is a fool part of the time—wisdom consists in not exceeding your time limit.

On July 29, 1978, Penny Dean set a new record for swimming the English Channel—7 hours, 42 minutes.

Peter's Fanatical Principle: Most public-opinion polls have a category for the undecided, but they should also have a category for the overdecided.

COPPERHEAD DAY

IN THE *Cincinnati Gazette* of July 30, 1862, during the Civil War, the term "copperhead" was first used to designate a Northerner who was sympathetic to the Southern cause. A copperhead is also the name of a venomous snake. The label was not meant to be a compliment.

When the meek inherit the earth and pay the inheritance tax, capital gains, and legal fees in order to take over the world and its problems—the meek might still be losers.

On July 30, 1919, Fred Hoenemann, a farmer in Missouri, got an injunction prohibiting pilots from flying their planes over his barn. Many farmers had claimed that the flying machines disturbed livestock.

It costs more to live now than ever before—but it's still worth it.

On July 30, 1619, the first representative assembly in America, the Virginia General Assembly, met in Jamestown, Virginia.

Peter's Promotion Principle: Advertising makes you think you've wanted something all your life that you never heard of before.

SAXOPHONE
LIBERATION DAY

ON JULY 31, 1845, the saxophone, invented by the Belgian musical instrument maker Adolf Sax five years earlier, was officially introduced into the military bands of the French Army.

The IRS should be grateful that we taxpayers have what it takes.

On July 31, 1947, the Smugglers' Union in Hendaze, France, went on strike protesting the laxity of customs guards in allowing citizens to bring fruit and wine across the Spanish-French border. The union claimed this was "sabotaging the smuggling business."

To mediocrity, genius is the one unforgivable sin.

On July 31, 1790, the first United States patent ever granted was issued to Samuel Hopkins of Vermont for a potash process.

Peter's Revised Timetable Principle: The big difficulties of life should come when we are 18 and know everything.

August

NATIONAL NON-PARENT DAY *August 1*

THE OBJECTIVE OF the August 1 National Non-Parent Day is to increase awareness of voluntary childlessness and promote recognition of the value of the child-free life-style. This day emphasizes the contribution to society made by those who choose the option of remaining child free.

If you're really mad, take a lesson from the space program—count down before blasting off.

On August 1, 1935, the Georgia Board of Education ordered all black teachers in the state holding membership in the National Association for the Advancement of Colored People to resign from that organization by September 15 or have their teaching licenses revoked for "life."

The more civilized the more helpless we are when there's an electric power failure.

Maria Mitchell, United States astronomer, the first female member of the Academy of Arts and Sciences, was born on August 1, 1818.

Peter's Confidence Principle: You can step in front of a moving vehicle and feel perfectly safe—if you are sure it's moving backward.

ON AUGUST 2, 1858, street letter boxes for depositing mail were set up in New York and Boston. Although the use of these devices had started in Belgium in 1848, it took ten years for the idea to be adopted in America.

If you have tact you'll have less to retract.

On August 2, 1936, Jesse Owens, with a time of 0:10:2, set a new world's record for the 100-meter run in the Olympic Games at Berlin, Germany.

A taxi is a vehicle that disappears when it rains.

August 2 is the Declaration of Independence signing anniversary. Contrary to the widespread misconception, the 56 signers did not sign as a group and did not do so on July 4, 1776. The official event took place on August 2, 1776, when 50 signed. The rest signed later.

Peter's Safety Rule: Never scratch a tiger with a short stick.

ON FRIDAY, AUGUST 3, 1492, Christopher Columbus, "Admiral of the Ocean Sea," set sail before sunrise from Palos, Spain, with three ships, *Niña, Pinta,* and *Santa Maria.* With a crew of 90 he sailed for Cathay, but instead landed in the New World of the Americas on San Salvador Island in the Bahamas.

Technology moves so fast that by the time we can afford the best there's something better.

On August 3, 1951, scandal rocked the U.S. Military Academy at West Point, New York, when authorities dismissed 90 cadets, including most of the members of the football team, for cheating on examinations.

Truth is stranger than fiction and more embarrassing.

On August 3, 1554, the earliest letter in Europe known to be sealed with sealing wax was sent by Rheingrave Philip Francis von Daun in Germany to his agent in England, Gerrard Herman.

Peter's Immutable Information Rule: No news is no news.

ON AUGUST 4, 1790, the United States was provided with its first naval protection when the Revenue Cutter Service was organized by an act of the first Congress. Alexander Hamilton, first Secretary of the Treasury, was authorized to develop a ten-ship antismuggling fleet at a cost not to exceed $10,000. The service received the name Coast Guard on January 28, 1915.

If you want to learn to drive, I won't stand in your way.

On August 4, 1944, in the center of Amsterdam, the Nazi police discovered a hidden room and captured Anne Frank and seven other Jews who had been concealed there for 756 days. All later died except Anne's father, who returned to the house after the war and found her diary. *The Diary of Anne Frank* has since been read by millions.

Three happy moments are when you get the last laugh, have the last word, and pay the last installment.

On August 4, 1916, the United States bought the Virgin Islands, formerly the Danish West Indies, from Denmark, with the transfer to take place on March 31, 1917.

Peter's Age-of-Discretion Principle: You know that you've passed the dangerous age when your name appears in the obituary column.

FEDERAL INCOME TAX BIRTHDAY

ON AUGUST 5, 1861, Abraham Lincoln signed into law the first federal income-tax law. It came into effect January 1, 1862, and levied a 3 percent tax on incomes over $800. It was an emergency wartime measure that was rescinded in 1872.

You can always enjoy television if you have a big enough screen—just put it in front of the set.

On August 5, 1876, "Wild Bill Hickok," a United States marshall, was killed in a saloon in Deadwood, South Dakota, by Jack McCall in revenge for his brother's death at Hickok's hands.

The only thing a teenager will take lying down is a telephone call.

On August 5, 1780, Benedict Arnold, a traitor dealing with the British, was put in charge of the West Point fort in New York during the American Revolutionary War.

Peter's Intoxication Rule: Remember the floor is your safety zone—you can't fall off it.

FIRST SOUND MOTION PICTURE SHOWING

ON APRIL 6, 1926, two short-subject films produced by Warner Bros. were shown at the Warner Theatre in New York. The first film had clear sound and presented the New York Philharmonic-Symphony Orchestra and the voices of Marion Talley, Anna Chase, and Giovanni Martinelli. The second film presented John Barrymore and other actors whose voices were inaudible.

Engagement has two meanings—in war, it's a battle; in courtship, it's a surrender.

August 6, 1945, saw the United States drop the first atomic bomb—on Hiroshima in Japan.

It's difficult for a politician to keep the note of envy out of his voice when accusing his opponent of fooling the public.

On August 6, 1978, Ardeth Evitt, 74, of Paris, Illinois, followed her grandson out of a plane at 3,000 feet and became the world's oldest woman parachute jumper.

Peter's Law of Office Procedure: You always have to dig for something in the wastebasket just after you empty the ash tray.

THE REVOLVING DOOR, a device that was useful in preventing large quantities of cold air from entering public buildings in winter, was patented by Theophilus Van Kannel of Philadelphia on August 7, 1888.

The best epigrams, like other inventions, annoy us because we didn't think of them ourselves.

On August 7, 1936, the U.S. Court of Appeals struck a heavy blow at censorship. It ruled against attempts to ban James Joyce's book *Ulysses*. The court pointed out that if the book could be banned for erotic passages, so could *Hamlet*, *Romeo and Juliet*, and the *Odyssey*.

All epigrams exaggerate—including this one.

On August 7, 1794, the Whiskey Rebellion in Western Pennsylvania, a protest against the tax on whiskey, resulted in President George Washington's calling out the army.

Peter's Last-Chance Rule: If you can't win, break even, or get out of the game, your only hope is to change the rules.

UNITED STATES DOLLAR DAY   *August 8*

ON AUGUST 8, 1786, the silver dollar and the decimal system of money were adopted by an act of Congress: "That the money unit of the United States of America be one dollar—that the several pieces shall increase in decimal ratio—that the smallest coin be a copper, of which 200 shall pay for one dollar."

Television has changed the American child from an irresistible force to an immovable object.

On August 8, 1923, Benny Goodman, 14 years old, was hired for his first professional job as a clarinetist with the band on a Chicago excursion boat.

I was confined to the house with a bad haircut.

On August 8, 1963, bandits robbed a train near London of $7 million, accomplishing the biggest train robbery in history.

Peter's Feminist Principle: Most hierarchies were established by men who now monopolize the upper levels, thus depriving women of their rightful share of opportunities for incompetence.

ON AUGUST 9, 1936, at the Olympic Games in Germany, Jesse Owens, a black American track star, confounded Nazi Germany's white supremacy propaganda by becoming the first man to win four Olympic gold medals.

You don't get rid of a bad temper by losing it.

On August 9, 1945, the United States dropped the second atomic bomb, this time on Nagasaki.

An executive is the person who is always annoying the hired help by asking them to do things.

On August 9, 1831, the first American train drawn by a steam locomotive made a run between Albany and Schenectady, New York.

Peter's Theory of Aeronautic Design: Every aircraft has two ends—the end where I sit and the end where they start serving the drinks.

GREENWICH OBSERVATORY DAY

ON AUGUST 10, 1675, on the order of Charles II, construction began on the world's most famous astronomical observatory, at Greenwich, England, the center from which the world's time is regulated. At the time of construction its main function was to improve astronomical observations for navigation.

If you have trouble making both ends meet—get a longer belt.

On August 10, 1833, Chicago was incorporated as a village with a population of about 200.

Everyone prefers to learn certain things by personal experience— like the proverb that money does not bring happiness.

Carrie Jacobs Bond, songwriter whose 1910 hit "A Perfect Day" sold over 5 million copies, was born August 10, 1862.

Peter's Law of Selective Gravitation: Any dropped object will land where it will (1) be of maximum inconvenience, (2) do the most damage, or (3) roll to the most inaccessible location.

FEAST OF SAINT CLARE OF ASSISI

SAINT CLARE was received into the austere religious life by Francis of Assisi himself, to become the first and most famous member of the Franciscan order, and the founder of the Second Order of St. Francis, an order of women Franciscans. The Feast of Saint Clare is observed by Roman Catholics and some Episcopalians on August 11, the date of her death in 1253.

Some thirst after fame, some thirst after power, but we all thirst after salted peanuts.

On August 11, 1902, Oliver Wendell Holmes was appointed associate justice of the U.S. Supreme Court by President Theodore Roosevelt.

Experience is the best teacher—because everyone gets individual instruction.

On August 11, 1928, Herbert Hoover failed to foresee the Great Depression when he stated, "We in America today are nearer the final triumph over poverty than ever before in the history of any land."

Peter's Humanist Principle: Religion, government, and the military cannot stand the idea of the human race being a success, because then they would be unnecessary.

ON AUGUST 12, 1877, Thomas A. Edison turned over the crude model of his "talking machine" (phonograph) to an assistant, John Kreusi, with instructions to make a finished working model for demonstration. Mr. Kreusi was skeptical and said, "Next you will make one to think and eat, I suppose. But, I bet you, Mr. Edison, I bet you two dollars that it won't work." When the talking machine worked, Edison reminded him of the bet and collected the two dollars.

The only food for thought is more thought.

On August 11, 1851, Isaac Singer obtained a patent for his sewing machine and with capital of $40 started in business in Boston.

My TV gave me a lot of pleasure this summer—I swapped it for an air-conditioner.

On August 12, 1918, the first regular airmail service between Washington, D.C., and New York City was established by the U.S. Post Office.

Peter's Petrol Principle: Never give a sucker a siphon hose.

LUCY STONE, born on August 13, 1819, became the leading suffragist and abolitionist of the nineteenth century. She was still a child when she became indignant about the second-class treatment of women. She became a person of unusual personal persuasiveness and the first to stir the heart of the American public on the woman question. She achieved notoriety by her determination to assert her individuality by retaining her family name after marriage. Women who followed her example were called Lucy Stoners.

If you have trouble making the ends of your tie come out even— wear a vest.

On August 13, 1930, Captain Frank Hawks set a new speed record when he flew from Los Angeles to New York in 12 hours 25 minutes.

Experience is like drawing without an eraser.

On August 13, 1587, an American Indian, Maneo, became the first of his race to be converted to Protestantism and baptized into the Church of England.

Peter's Joy-of-Walking Principle: Long walks are very beneficial, especially when taken by visiting relatives.

ON AUGUST 14, 1457, the first printed book was published by Faust, a wandering astrologer. It was the Book of Psalms, a section of the Bible he had begun in 1450. He offered some copies for sale in Paris, where he was thrown in prison on suspicion that he was working with the devil, for the French could not understand how books could agree exactly in every detail without the devil's assistance. To prove his innocence Faust had to disclose his secret. This adventure is the basis of many ludicrous dialogues between Faust (Dr. Faustus) and the devil in the dramas by Goethe and Marlowe.

There's nothing wrong with teenagers that trying to reason with them won't aggravate.

On August 14, 1935, Congress passed the Social Security Act establishing old-age and unemployment benefits.

Experience is the best teacher—but you learn things you don't want to know.

On August 14, 1945, Japan surrendered (VJ Day) ending World War II. The formal surrender ceremonies were held on September 2.

Peter's Life-style Principle: Living life in the fast lane means you can only afford ten items.

AUGUST 15 is named for Nicolas Chauvin, a French soldier who idolized Napoleon to the degree that he eventually became a subject of ridicule for his blind loyalty to everything French. Chauvinism has come to mean blind or absurdly intense attachment to any cause.

Tolerance is what enables the rich to declare that there is no disgrace in being poor.

On August 15, 1914, the Panama Canal was officially opened as the ship *Ancon* traveled from the Atlantic to the Pacific through the canal.

Eating dried beef is jerky.

On August 15, 1935, Will Rogers and Wiley Post died in a plane crash near Point Barrow, Alaska.

Peter's Perfect-Fit Principle: The nice thing about a pair of slacks is when they have no slack.

ON AUGUST 16, 1896, great excitement followed the discovery of gold in the Klondike at Bonanza Creek, Alaska, and the gold rush was on.

How do you determine just when to discard a toothbrush?

On August 17, 1923, steelworkers applauded the Carnegie Steel Corporation's decision to establish the eight-hour work-day.

Conservatism is a step in the right direction.

On August 16, 1776, Horace Walpole said, "This world is a comedy to those that think, a tragedy to those that feel."

Peter's United Principle: An organization with "united" in its name, means it isn't, as in United Nations, United Arab Republic, United Kingdom, and United States.

ON AUGUST 17, 1978, three Americans, Maxie Anderson, Ben Abruzzo, and Larry Newman, became the first to complete a transatlantic trip by balloon. In their balloon *Double Eagle II*, they left Presque Isle, Maine, August 11, traveled 3,120 miles in 137 hours, 3 minutes, and landed at Miserey, France, near Paris.

Art opens our eyes to the possibilities—modern art to the impossibilities.

On August 17, 1790, New York ended its role as the federal capital as the government moved to Philadelphia. At various times the capital has been New York, Philadelphia, York, Lancaster, Baltimore, Annapolis, Trenton, Princeton, and finally Washington, D.C.

To me it's the motor that's knocking—to the mechanic it's opportunity.

On August 17, 1807, Robert Fulton's steamboat *Clermont* set out from New York on its maiden voyage up the Hudson River to Albany.

Peter's Fashion Principle: It is not essential to buy each new style in order to look ridiculous every season.

VIRGINIA DARE DAY   *August 18*

ON AUGUST 18, 1587, Virginia Dare was born, the first child of English parents to be born in the New World. She was born to Ellinor and Ananias Dare of Roanoke Island.

Space travel is out of this world.

On August 18, 1963, James H. Meredith graduated from the University of Mississippi without incident. He was the first black to receive a degree in the 115-year history of the university. Just 11 months earlier his enforced admission had provoked race riots.

An argument usually consists of two people each trying to get the last word—first.

On August 18, 1919, the Anti-Cigarette League of America was organized in Chicago.

Peter's Safety Principle: There is no safety in numbers, or anything else.

By Presidential Proclamation Franklin D. Roosevelt established the anniversary of Orville Wright's birthday, August 19, 1871, as National Aviation Day. Orville Wright piloted the first powered flight of an airplane, the *Kitty Hawk*.

Tolerance is the belief that those who disagree with you have a right to be wrong.

On August 19, 1890, the Daughters of the American Revolution was formed. The organization consisted of women with at least one ancestor who aided in American independence.

Abstract art is proof that things aren't as bad as they're painted.

On August 19, 1812, the United States frigate *Constitution* (Old Ironsides) fought its victorious battle with the British frigate *Guerrière*. The British had ridiculed the *Constitution* as "a bundle of pine boards sailing under a bit of striped bunting."

Peter's Equalization Theory: The only place where you can be on dead level with others is in a cemetery.

ON AUGUST 20, 1929, the first all-black-cast movie, *Hallelujah*, was released.

The best travel slogan still is "Let yourself go."

On August 20, 1964, President Lyndon B. Johnson signed the "antipoverty bill" as a first step aimed at creating The Great Society. He said, ". . . The days of the dole in our country are numbered . . ."

A newcomer to New York visited the Metropolitan Museum of Art and watched a class of students copying original paintings. Finally the visitor asked one of the young artists, "What do they do with the old pictures when you get the new ones finished?"

On August 20, 1940, Prime Minister Winston Churchill, paying tribute to the Royal Air Force, made his famous statement to the House of Commons, "Never was so much owed by so many to so few."

Peter's Intelligence Rule: Half of being smart is knowing what you're dumb at.

HAWAII ADMISSION DAY   *August 21*

ON AUGUST 21, 1959, a new state was admitted into the Union as President Eisenhower officially proclaimed Hawaii the fiftieth state of the United States and a new 50-star flag was unfurled at the White House.

Don't bore your friends with your troubles, tell them to your enemies—they'll enjoy hearing about them.

August is the month when you can't open the bus window that you can't close in December.

It's better to tighten your belt than to lose your pants.

On August 21, 1621, 12 young women were sent from England to Virginia to be sold as wives. The price was 120 pounds of tobacco each, or approximately one pound of tobacco for one pound of woman.

Peter's Automotive Principle: No matter how much you pay for your car, once you leave the lot it's just an assembly of used parts.

On August 22, 1851, the yacht *America*, built by a group of members of the New York Yacht Club, was entered in a race against 14 yachts belonging to the Royal Yacht Squadron. The race around the Isle of Wight was won by the *America*. The winning of this event was the reason for establishing the America's Cup sailing challenge.

The only friends you can really trust are the ones who never ask you to trust them.

I think that child psychology would work if we could just get the children to understand it.

Of two evils, choose the one least likely to be talked about.

On August 22, 1865, William Sheppard received a United States patent for making liquid soap consisting of a mixture of ordinary soap and ammonia.

Peter's Smoker Principle: If you think you are dying for a cigarette, you probably are.

ON AUGUST 23, 1859, the first elevator was installed in the six-story Fifth Avenue Hotel in New York City.

Maybe you can't take it with you, but just try to travel without it.

On August 23, 1923, the first real comedians of radio broadcasting, Billy Jones and Ernie Hare, went on the air for the Happiness Candy Company, billed as "The Happiness Boys."

Children are natural mimics—they imitate their parents in spite of every effort to teach them to behave properly.

On August 23, 1500, in Haiti, Christopher Columbus was arrested and ordered sent back to Spain in chains because of accusations of mistreating the natives.

Peter's Perception Principle: It is easier to see the difference between ourselves and our inferiors than it is to see the difference between ourselves and our superiors.

FIRST FEMALE TRANSCONTINENTAL FLIGHT

ON AUGUST 23, 1932, Amelia Earhart became the first woman to make a transcontinental nonstop flight, starting from Los Angeles, California, and landing in Newark, New Jersey, a distance of 2,600 miles with a flying time of 19 hours, 5 minutes.

There is nothing that proves human capacity for tolerance as does a golden wedding anniversary.

You don't realize how many of your old school chums have become highbrows until they remove their hats.

At the university we had a dean who was so dumb that even the other deans noticed it.

On August 24, 1869, Cornelius Swartout patented the waffle iron in the United States.

Peter's Agreement Principle: I'm not always right, but those that disagree with me are always wrong.

ON AUGUST 25, 1830, a race took place between a locomotive named *Tom Thumb* and a horse-drawn vehicle. The horse-drawn vehicle won when the locomotive broke down.

Truth is stranger than fiction—but not nearly as convincing.

On August 25, 1718, the city of New Orleans, Louisiana, was founded. It was named in honor of the Duke of Orléans in France.

Old college presidents never die—they just lose their faculties.

On August 25, 1916, the National Park Service was established within the U.S. Department of the Interior.

Peter's Humility Principle: It is wise to remember that you are one of those who can be fooled some of the time.

WOMEN'S EQUALITY DAY   *August 26*

AUGUST 26 IS THE ANNIVERSARY of the adoption of the Nine-teenth Amendment in 1920, prohibiting discrimination on the basis of sex with regard to voting: "The right of citizens of the United States to vote shall not be denied or abridged by the United States or by any state on account of sex."

Ugliness is a point of view—an ulcer may be beautiful to a pathologist.

My daughter said, "Jim is a perfect gentleman at all times—but I guess that's better than having no boyfriend at all."

They say that a camel looks like a horse designed by a committee—no committee ever came up with any design as unique and as functional as a camel.

On August 26, 1873, Dr. Lee De Forest was born. In 1906 he invented the three-element vacuum tube making modern elec-tronic technology, radio, and television possible.

Peter's Status Principle: In a democracy you can be respected even though you are poor—as long as they don't find out.

AMERICAN PETROLEUM DAY *August 27*

ON AUGUST 27, 1859, Colonel Edwin L. Drake drilled the first successful oil well in the United States near Titusville, Pennsylvania. This was the beginning of the development of the American petroleum industry.

The trouble with tolerance is that people will think you don't understand the problem.

On August 27, 550 B.C., Confucius, the great Chinese philosopher, was born.

Tell someone there are 300 billion stars in the universe and he'll believe you. Tell him the bench has just been painted and he'll feel it to check you out.

On August 27, 1938, at a poetry reading by Archibald MacLeish, a jealous Robert Frost set fire to some papers to disrupt the performance.

Peter's Contentment Principle: Peace of mind is difficult when the past haunts us, the future taunts us, and the present flaunts us.

ON AUGUST 28 at the Grand Hotel, Mackinac Island, Michigan, a sauntering event is held annually. The objective is to revive the forgotten art of Victorian sauntering and discourage jogging. Certificates are awarded and nominations for the Sauntering Hall of Fame are accepted.

The problem with success is that its formula is the same as the one for ulcers.

On August 28, 1833, the British Parliament banned slavery throughout the empire.

All it takes for an argument is two loud mouths and four deaf ears.

On August 28, 1963, approximately 200,000 people staged a peaceful civil-rights march on Washington, D.C.

Peter's Ego Principle: The first madman to have someone imagine he was Napoleon was Napoleon.

ACCORDING TO HOYLE DAY   *August 29*

AUGUST 29 IS THE DAY to remember Edmond Hoyle and a day for fun and games according to the rules. Little is known about Hoyle's life but it is believed that he studied law. His birth date and birthplace are unknown. He lived in London and gave lessons on playing games. He wrote a paper, published in 1742, on playing whist. His name became synonymous with correct play and the phrase "according to Hoyle" became part of the English language.

There are many ways to get high blood pressure—one of which is mountain climbing over molehills.

On August 29, 1957, Senator Strom Thurmond, filibustering over the Civil Rights Bill, gave the longest speech on record—24 hours, 18 minutes. In spite of his efforts, the bill passed.

> Early to bed, early to rise.
> Work like hell, and advertise.

On August 29, 1896, chop suey was introduced at a restaurant in New York City, not in China, although it became a mainstay of Chinese restaurants.

Peter's Authorship Principle: Anybody can write, but authors are the people who can't do anything else.

GAS AND ELECTRIC CAR DAY *August 30*

ON AUGUST 30, 1929, Colonel E. H. Green took delivery of a newly designed combination gas and electric automobile built by the General Electric Company of Schenectady, New York. It was a 60-horsepower vehicle that had no clutch or gear shift. Two pedals, one on each side of the central brake pedal, were used for acceleration.

Half the people are unhappy because they don't have the things that are making the other half unhappy.

On August 30, 30 B.C., Cleopatra committed suicide by holding an asp to her breast and permitting it to bite her.

Socrates was accused of being an atheist for proposing that there is only one god.

On August 30, 1963, a direct "hot line" was established between the White House in Washington and the Kremlin in Moscow.

Peter's Rules of Government Cost Overruns:
(1) It is too early to predict what the program will cost.
(2) It is too far down the road to do anything about it.

ON AUGUST 31, 1903, a Packard automobile ended a 52-day journey from San Francisco to New York, the first time an automobile had crossed the continent under its own power.

He said he didn't want to talk about his ulcer—it was a sore spot with him.

On August 31, 1955, Argentine President Juan Perón offered to resign from office in an effort to end political unrest. Later in the day, Perón withdrew this offer and told 100,000 followers in the Plaza de Mayo in Buenos Aires to "answer violence with greater violence."

Never do card tricks for your poker group.

On August 31, 1803, Lewis and Clark began their exploration of western America.

Peter's Negative Aspect of Positive Thinking: An optimist can never be pleasantly surprised.

September

If we fail to understand the nature of freedom, this most vital, human, and precious possession, we may destroy its source— our habitat. We will never build a spaceship as beautiful as earth, never one so suited to our needs, never one with such potential for our true progress toward fulfillment of our highest humanity.

LAURENCE J. PETER,
from *The Peter Plan*

END OF WORLD WAR II DAY   *September 1*

WORLD WAR II, which had begun in Europe on September 1, 1939, with the invasion of Poland by Nazi Germany, ended six years later to the day, September 1, 1945. The final concluding ceremony came the following day, September 2, 1945, with the signing of surrender papers by representatives of Japan, Nazi Germany's Axis partner in the Far East.

You can't change the past, but you can ruin the present by worrying about the future.

September 1 is the first day of Emergency Care Month, a time to educate the public in performance of emergency medical practices, to enable individuals to administer lifesaving care before professional medical help arrives, and to pay tribute to those skilled in emergency medical care.

Children help to keep a family together—especially when you can't get a baby-sitter.

On September 1, 1878, Emma Nutt became America's first female telephone operator. Within a few hours her sister became the second.

Peter's Parenting Principle: You've just got to have problems when children are raised by young people who have no experience as parents.

THIS DAY COMMEMORATES the birth of the American author Henry George, September 2, 1839. His most important books were *Our Land and Land Policy* (1871) and *Progress and Poverty* (1879). As an economist and land reformer he had a large following and his books sold millions of copies. His utopian idea was based on the concept of the "margin of productivity" as it applied to land alone. Since economic progress entailed the growing scarcity of land, the idle landowner reaped greater returns at the expense of the productive factors of labor and capital. He held that this unearned economic rent should be taxed away by the state. Government income from this single tax would be so large there would be a surplus for expansion of public works and services. His arguments had great humanitarian and religious appeal.

Much unhappiness is caused by the belief that other people are happy.

An eccentric is a person who is too rich to be called a crackpot.

On September 2, 1789, the U.S. Treasury Department was established by Congress.

Peter's Miss America Principle: Never trust a contest where the winner cries and the losers smile.

SEPTEMBER 3, 1752 never happened in England, nor did the 10 days that should have followed it. When the Gregorian calendar was adopted on September 2, 1752, it was required to make an adjustment that dropped 11 days. This decision caused riots because the people thought that the government had stolen 11 days of their lives.

All member states of the United Nations have one thing in common—the ability to see one another's faults.

I remember when a liberal was a person who was generous with his own money.

I enjoy reading the ancient magazines in my doctor's office—it gives me a sense of security to know he has been in practice so long.

On September 3, 1852, the London *Times*, in commenting on the great popularity in London of Harriet Beecher Stowe's novel *Uncle Tom's Cabin* said, "Mrs. Stowe has received 10,000 pounds as her copyright premium on three months' sales of the work—we believe the largest sum of money ever received by any author, either American or European, from the sale of a single work in so short a period of time."

Peter's Solvency Principle: You can't live within your income if you don't consider it a living.

ON SEPTEMBER 4, 1833, Barney Flaherty, a ten-year-old New York boy, became the first newsboy in the United States when he was hired by the publisher of the *New York Sun*.

Nature abhors a vacuum so she fills empty heads with conceit.

On September 4, 1885, the Exchange Buffet, an early form of cafeteria, opened in New York City at 7 New Street.

The young tell us what they are doing, the old what they have done, and the rest of us what we are going to do.

On September 4, 1888, George Eastman patented the first roll-film camera and registered the name Kodak.

Peter's Primary Principle: When two people go to bed together at the same time, the one that snores will go to sleep first.

SEPTEMBER 5 is sponsored by the Procrastinators' Club of America as Be Late for Something Day to create a relief from the stress and strain caused by the constant need to be on time.

A rut is a grave with the ends knocked out.

On September 5, 1885, Sylvester F. Bowser of Fort Wayne, Indiana, who had built the first gasoline pump, delivered it to Jake D. Gumper, a gasoline dealer.

An atheist is someone who believes that what you see is what you get—someone who believes fervently in disbelief.

On August 5, 1921, the Chamber of Commerce of Richmond, Virginia, petitioned for the renaming of Main Street because of the bad image created by the Sinclair Lewis novel.

Peter's Theory of the Political Promise: If the government promises you something, it must first take it from you.

ON SEPTEMBER 6, 1923, United States piano manufacturers announced that player pianos were in great demand all over the United States. At least half the new pianos were player pianos operated by foot pedals turning perforated paper rolls. Americans bought nearly 350,000 pianos that year.

They make you start school when you can't read or write and then tell you not to talk.

On September 6, 1862, General Stonewall Jackson ordered his Confederate soldiers to fire on the Union flag in Barbara Frietchie's attic window. This incident is the basis for Whittier's poem about Barbara Frietchie.

America is a country that doesn't know where it is going—but is determined to set a speed record in getting there.

On September 6, 1837, women students at Oberlin Collegiate Institute (now Oberlin College) were granted equal status with men, making it the first coeducational institution of higher learning in the country.

Peter's Advertising Principle: Advertising is the art of making whole lies out of half truths.

CARNEGIE LIBRARY DAY   *September 7*

ON SEPTEMBER 7, 1866, the Lord Provost of Edinburgh announced at a meeting of the town council that Mr. Andrew Carnegie of New York had increased his offer of 25,000 pounds for a free library for Edinburgh to 50,000 pounds.

Virtue is learned at mother's knee—vice at other joints.

On September 7, 1899, in Newport, Rhode Island, 19 automobiles participated in the first automobile parade to be held in this country.

Football is a fascinating game in which 22 men fight to get a ball that doesn't even bounce right.

On September 7, 1892, in New Orleans, James J. Corbett won the heavyweight boxing championship from John L. Sullivan in the first championship bout held under the Marquis of Queensberry rules.

Peter's Laughter Law: It's hard to create humor because of the unfair competition from the real world.

INTERNATIONAL LITERACY DAY

SEPTEMBER 8 is observed by the organization of the United Nations as a day of international commitment to literacy.

War never determines who is right—just who is left.

On September 8, 1978, the City Council of Woonsocket, Rhode Island, approved an amendment that changed the title of "utility man" to "utility person," and the job of building "manholes" to building "personholes." Embarrassed by national publicity, on September 19, 1978, the council dropped the new term "person-holes" but kept "utility person."

I inherited my ability from both parents—my mother's ability for spending money and my father's ability at not making it.

On September 8, 1939, at the *Gone with the Wind* preview, producer David O. Selznick counted the people using the restroom during the movie. With this information he won the decision to add an intermission.

Peter's Value Principle: Nearly everything is marginally better than daytime TV.

UNITED STATES DAY   *September 9*

ON SEPTEMBER 9, 1776, the term *United States* became official as the Second Continental Congress ruled ". . . that in all Continental commissions and other instruments where heretofore the words 'United Colonies' have been used, the style be altered, for the future, to the 'United States.'"

Once upon a time only Washington's face was on our money—now Washington's hands are on it too.

I visited Washington—to see the people I'm working for and to be near my money.

One of the few things you can still get for a dollar is an engraved picture of George Washington.

September 9 is California Admission Day, commemorating its admission to the United States as the thirty-first state, on this day in 1850.

―――――――――――

Peter's Theory of Full Employment: Many Americans are not working, but fortunately most of them have jobs.

THE INTERNATIONAL SOCIETY for Philosophical Enquiry has identified September 10 as the day to encourage people to explore ways ideas can be put to work for the benefit of humanity and to develop incentives to encourage use of creative imagination.

There is one thing wrong with a watch that is waterproof, shockproof, and antimagnetic—you can still lose it.

On the evening of September 10, 1739, R. Thomas Sheridan, the Irish classical scholar, was discussing the direction of the wind with a friend. He said, "Let the wind blow east, west, north, or south, the immortal soul will take its flight to the destined point." He then leaned back in his chair and died.

Everyone can serve some useful service—for example, a miser makes a wonderful ancestor.

On September 10, 1978, Americans celebrated the first national Grandparents' Day, after President Jimmy Carter signed the proclamation.

Peter's Utopian Principle: A welfare state is one that assumes responsibility for the health, happiness, and general well-being of all its citizens—except the taxpayer.

SEPTEMBER 11 is a time to observe the neighborhood as a vital national asset and to celebrate the accomplishments of neighborhood organizations.

The tragedy of war is that it sacrifices our best to achieve our worst.

On September 11, 1847, the proprietor of Andres' Eagle Ice Cream Saloon in Pittsburgh, Pennsylvania, advertised in the Pittsburgh *Daily Commercial Journal* that entertainers in his emporium would sing Stephen Foster's "Oh! Susanna" that evening, the first public performance of the song.

The Bible contains much that is relevant today—like Noah's taking 40 days to find a place to park.

On September 11, 1927, an American meat-packer announced the production of a frankfurter with a zipper, and advised "boil the hot dog in its zippered casing and then discard it." How many followed these instructions and threw away the hot dog and kept the casing was not reported.

Peter's Rumor Principle: If you hadn't said it they wouldn't have repeated it.

CEDARS OF LEBANON DAY   *September 12*

ON SEPTEMBER 12, 1881, the Turkish governor of Lebanon issued an ordinance for the protection of the remaining 400 trees of the once extensive forest of cedars. A wall was built around the trees and a custodian appointed to protect them from the souvenir hunter's practice of cutting branches, thus saving the famous Cedars of Lebanon.

In modern warfare there are only two types of weapons—obsolete and experimental.

Beauty like truth and a contact lens is in the eye of the beholder.

A book on your shelf is a friend that turns its back on you and remains your friend.

On September 12, 1866, the opening of the New York stage show, *The Black Crook,* marked the beginning of the era of girlie shows in the United States.

Peter's To-Err-Is-Human Principle: The inventor of the eraser had the human race pretty well sized up.

POSITIVE THINKING DAY   *September 13*

ON SEPTEMBER 13, 1872, George Francis Train, adventurer, newspaper publisher, railroader, world traveler, and presidential candidate, described his qualifications for the office: "I am that wonderful, eccentric, independent, extraordinary genius and political reformer of America, who is sweeping off all the politicans before him like a hurricane. I am your modest, diffident, unassuming friend, the future President of America—George Francis Train." In the November election he received no votes.

In the game of life, heredity deals the hand, society makes the rules, but you can still play your own cards.

A bore is someone endowed with more patience than his listeners.

Infant care has to be learned from the bottom up.

On September 13, 1931, Rudy Vallee introduced the song "Life Is Just a Bowl of Cherries," in a musical review in New York. It was the depth of the Depression when for millions life was just a bowl of pits.

Peter's Violence-in-Movies Principle: If it's worth doing—it's worth overdoing.

ON SEPTEMBER 14, 1886, George K. Anderson of Memphis, Tennessee, patented the typewriter ribbon.

You can become wise by noticing what happens when you aren't.

On September 14, 1741, the composer George Frederick Handel, having worked without interruption for 23 days, finished his *Messiah*.

The less you bet, the more you lose when you win.

This is also National Anthem Day. On September 14, 1814, at the bombardment of Fort McHenry in the War of 1812, Francis Scott Key wrote the words of "The Star Spangled Banner."

Peter's Bicycling Law: No matter which direction you go, it's uphill and against the wind.

SEPTEMBER 15 IS Old People's Day or Respect for the Aged Day. In Japan it is a national holiday.

Time makes a wise person wiser and a fool more foolish—but so does everything else.

September 15 is Felt Hat Day, the traditional day for men of fashion to put away their straw hats and resume wearing felt hats for the winter.

Censors are people who know more than they think you ought to.

Mexico Independence Day, September 15-16, marks the beginning of the successful revolution against Spanish colonial government in 1810.

Peter's Contentment Rules: (1) Encourage conformity. (2) Don't take chances. (3) Discourage Innovation. (4) Be satisfied with mediocrity.

MAYFLOWER DEPARTURE DAY

ON SEPTEMBER 16, 1620, after two previous false starts, the 102-pilgrims—74 men and 28 women—and a small crew set sail from Plymouth, England, aboard the *Mayflower* for the New World in search of religious freedom. The *Mayflower*, formerly a wine ship, reached Provincetown, Massachusetts, on December 26, 1620.

Brevity is the soul of wit, and laughter is the goal of it.

On September 16, 1901, aboard the funeral train of the late President William McKinley, the political boss Mark Hanna complained to the editor of the *Chicago Times Herald* that Theodore Roosevelt was now President. "I told William McKinley it was a mistake to nominate that wild man at Philadelphia. . . . Now look! That damn cowboy is President of the United States!"

A characteristic of the normal child is that he doesn't behave that way very often.

September 16, 1893, is also Cherokee Strip Day in Oklahoma. More than 100,000 homesteaders rushed the strip between Oklahoma and Kansas to claim shares of 6 million acres of land opened up to settlers by the United States government.

Peter's Immutable Principle: Natural laws have no pity.

THIS DAY IS OBSERVED each year, by Presidential Proclamation, on the anniversary of the adoption of the U.S. Constitution. On September 17, 1787, the Constitution of the United States was completed and signed by the majority of the 55 delegates attending the Constitutional Convention in Philadelphia. Delegates were sent from 12 of the original 13 colonies, Rhode Island failing to attend.

My wife said she never knew the value of education until the children went back to school.

Ben Turpin, the cross-eyed comic, born September 17, 1874, was the first movie actor to have a pie thrown in his face in a movie.

To an atheist, death is the end; to a believer, the beginning; to an agnostic, the sound of silence.

On September 17, 1796, in his farewell address, President George Washington wrote, "'Tis our true policy to steer clear of permanent alliances with any portion of the foreign world . . . . Harmony, and a liberal intercourse with all nations, are recommended by policy, humanity, and interest."

Peter's Theory of Professorial Infighting: Academics in higher education are so vicious because the stakes are so small.

ON SEPTEMBER 18, 1851, *The New York Times*, founded by George Jones and Henry Raymond, went on sale for 2 cents a copy.

One of the first things my son learned when he went to school was that other kids got bigger allowances than he did.

On September 18, 1769, the *Boston Gazette* reported that the first piano made in this country was a spinet manufactured by one John Harris.

The major flaw in democracy is that only the party out of power knows how to run the government.

On September 18, 1927, the Columbia Broadcasting System went on the air with a radio network of 16 stations.

Peter's Success Formula: Create problems for which only you have the answer.

ON SEPTEMBER 19, 1768, an advertisement appeared in the *Boston Gazette* that offered hope to those with frontal dental gaps. "Whereas many persons are so unfortunate as to lose their fore-teeth by accident and other ways, to their great detriment, not only in looks but speaking both in public and in private, this is to inform all such that they may have them replaced with artificial ones that look as well as natural, and answers the end of speaking to all intents, by Paul Revere, Goldsmith—near the head of Dr. Clarke's Wharf, Boston."

The hero of the next war should be whoever prevents it.

If you don't learn from your mistakes, there isn't much sense in making them.

A fanatic is a person who is highly enthusiastic about something in which you are not remotely interested.

On September 19, 1859, the famous Confederate war song "Dixie" was sung by the actor Daniel Decatur Emmett at Bryant's Minstrel Theatre in New York.

Peter's Sleep Prescription: Sleeping in the open air will cure insomnia—so will sleeping anywhere else.

THE FIRST MEETING of the National Research Council took place in New York City on September 20, 1916. It was formed at the request of President Woodrow Wilson for ". . . encouraging the investigation of natural phenomena . . ." for American business and national security. September 20 is also the anniversary of the first meeting of the American Association for the Advancement of Science in 1948.

Nothing is really work unless you would rather be doing something else.

On September 20, 1797, the United States frigate *Constitution* (Old Ironsides) was launched at the Boston Navy Yard.

A democracy is where you can say what you think—even if you don't think.

On September 20, 1519, Portuguese explorer Ferdinand Magellan began his pioneering voyage around the world, in the service of Spain. He died in the Philippines and never made it.

Peter's Ladder of Success Rule: Sincerity is the secret of success. Once you can fake that you're on your way.

ON SEPTEMBER 21, 1897, the editor of the *New York Sun* wrote one of the all-time favorite editorials titled "Is There a Santa Claus?" in response to eight-year-old Virginia O'Hanlon of New York who had written asking that question. "Yes, Virginia, there is a Santa Claus. He exists as certainly as love and generosity and devotion exist, and you know that they abound and give to your life its highest beauty and joy."

A sense of humor makes the world a comedy—a sense of honor, a tragedy.

There is one thing more painful than learning from experience, and that is not learning from experience.

A fool and his money are soon parted—but were sure lucky to get together in the first place.

On September 21, 1915, the mysterious massive stone structures at Stonehenge on Salisbury Plain, England, were sold at auction for 6,600 pounds to C.H.E. Chubb of Salisbury.

Peter's Principle of Proof: The proof of the pudding is in the amount of Maalox you take later.

BOSTON BAKED BEANS DAY   *September 22*

ON SEPTEMBER 22, 1908, in an article in the *New York Tribune* on Boston Baked Beans, the following calculation was included: "Taking the average height of a Bostonian at 5 feet, 6 inches, and the height of a beanpot at 10 inches, one can easily figure that a Bostonian in a year eats more than two and five-sevenths times his own height in baked beans and more than his own weight."

The only disadvantage to becoming wise is that you have to realize how foolish you have been.

On September 22, 1692, the last persons were hanged for witchcraft in the American colonies. More than 250 persons were arrested on charges of witchcraft, 19 of whom were hanged.

Liberty is always unfinished business.

On September 22, 1789, the U.S. Post Office was established.

Peter's Falsehood Principle: A simple, easily understood, believable lie is more acceptable than a complex, difficult truth.

THIS IS A DAY to recognize the importance of dogs in American politics. On September 23, 1944, President Franklin D. Roosevelt made his famous "Fala Speech" in which he talked about his much traveled terrier, Fala. On September 23, 1952, Vice-Presidential candidate Richard M. Nixon gave his politically influential "Checkers Speech" on national television and radio. In response to a disclosure that he had accepted an "expense fund" from 76 wealthy and prominent Californians, he refuted allegations of wrongdoing but said he was willing to return any gifts except a little black-and-white cocker spaniel, Checkers, that had been presented to his daughters. A picture of Checkers was then shown on the television screen. It was an emotional triumph. Eisenhower declared that Nixon had been found to be "clean as a hound's tooth" and as a team they went on to victory at the polls.

I never met a yesman I didn't like.

There are three kinds of friends—best friends, guest friends, and pest friends.

On September 23, 1912, the first Mack Sennett "Keystone Comedy" motion picture was released.

Peter's Directive: From each according to his inability. To each according to his greed.

ON SEPTEMBER 24, 1962, the Fifth Circuit Court of Appeals in New Orleans ordered the University of Mississippi to admit James H. Meredith, a black, to its student body.

Yesterday is experience, tomorrow is hope, and today is getting from one to the other as best we can.

On September 24, 1934, Babe Ruth made his farewell appearance as a regular player with the New York Yankees at Yankee Stadium, New York.

Some problems are so complex that you have to be highly intelligent and well informed just to be undecided about them.

September 24, 1869, was called Black Friday when the price of gold dropped, arousing financial panic. This was an aftermath of an attempt of Jay Gould and Jim Fisk to corner the United States gold market.

Peter's Mind-over-Matter Principle: The human brain is our Achilles' heel.

DISCOVERY OF THE PACIFIC OCEAN DAY

ON SEPTEMBER 25, 1513, Vasco Nuñez de Balboa, a Spanish conquistador, became the first European to look at the Pacific Ocean. He led an expedition across the Panama Isthmus to the peaceful (Pacific) ocean and waded into it with drawn sword, symbolically taking it for Spain.

You are only young once—but if you do it right, once is enough.

On September 25, 1890, Congress established Yosemite National Park in California.

Congress favors a stable government, judging from all the stalling and horsing around it does.

On September 25, 1690, the first American newspaper, *Publick Occurrences*, was published in Boston. No second edition appeared because the publisher incurred the displeasure of the Royal Governor.

Peter's Theory of Name Selection: Every Tom, Dick, and Harry is named Bob.

MEDICAL
REGISTRATION DAY

September 26

ON SEPTEMBER 26, 1772, the New Jersey legislature passed a bill forbidding the practice of medicine without a license. The new law made exceptions of those who pulled teeth, drew blood, or gave free medical advice.

My wife says that school days were the happiest days of her life—once the children were old enough to attend.

On September 26, 1914, the U.S. Federal Trade Commission was established.

Affairs of state are conducted so that one generation pays the debts of the last generation by issuing bonds payable by the next generation.

On September 26, 1892, John Philip Sousa and his band presented their first public concert, playing Sousa's "Liberty Bell March."

Peter's Prediction: You will never be as sick as just before you stop breathing.

ANCESTOR APPRECIATION DAY — *September 27*

SEPTEMBER 27 IS A DAY designated for the expression of gratitude for one's personal existence. It is a time to pause for solemn reflection and appreciation of one's personal ancestral history.

The problem is how do you teach college students what they think they already know?

A liberal calls it share-the-wealth—a conservative calls it soak-the-rich.

I'm not greedy, all I want is the land next to mine.

On September 27, 1904, a New York policeman shouting "You can't do that on Fifth Avenue!" arrested a woman he had observed smoking a cigarette in the rear of an automobile on New York's famous street.

Peter's Aim-High Rule: Spit on the ceiling—anyone can spit on the floor.

THOMAS DAY, AN EDUCATOR, was a follower of Rousseau's revolutionary doctrines. Having decided that only a wife trained by the proper methods would suit him, he took two girls who were 12 years old from a foundling hospital in London and trained them to be perfect wives. He was a better dreamer than teacher and eventually gave the grown girls to husbands of their choice, along with hefty dowries. Trying to create the perfect woman wasn't his only educational failure. On September 28, 1789, he was killed by a kick from a horse he was training by a new method.

No matter how old you are, you are younger than you'll ever be.

On September 28, 1850, the flogging of sailors in the U.S. Navy was abolished.

If at first you don't succeed—try a little ardor.

On September 28, 1920, a grand jury in Chicago indicted eight members of the Chicago White Sox team for "throwing" the 1919 World Series to Cincinnati in what was called the "Black Sox Scandal."

Peter's Value System: Any proposal that can survive a bureaucratic feasibility study isn't worth doing.

XENOPHOBE
UNDERSTANDING DAY

September 29

SEPTEMBER 29 IS IDENTIFIED as Xenophobe Understanding Day to further the acceptance and understanding of Xenophobe persons who have an inordinate fear of strangers, especially foreigners. Today research leading to discovery of a cure for this phobia should be encouraged. Introduce yourself to a Xenophobe today.

Nothing has done more to bring husbands and wives together than dresses that zip up the back.

On September 29, 1902, David Belasco, the theatrical impresario, opened his own theatre in New York.

May your happiest days of the past be your saddest days of your future.

September 29 is Michaelmas Day and is celebrated as the feast of Saint Michael the Archangel.

Peter's Law of Success II: Be nice to people until you make a million—then they'll be nice to you.

ON SEPTEMBER 30, 1846, Dr. William Morton, a dentist in Charlestown, Massachusetts, extracted a tooth for the first time with the help of anesthesia. He recorded the episode: "Toward evening, a man residing in Boston came in, suffering great pain, and wishing to have a tooth extracted. He was afraid of the operation, and asked if he could be mesmerized. I told him I had something better and saturated my handkerchief with ether and gave it to him to inhale. He became unconscious almost immediately. It was dark, and Dr. Hayden held the lamp while I extracted a firmly rooted bicuspid tooth . . . . He recovered in a minute and knew nothing of what had been done for him."

The most effective way to stop student protests would be to make them a required course.

Man can live without air for seconds, without water for days, without food for weeks, and without ideas for years.

You don't know what you know until you know what you don't know.

Peter's Law of Irrelevance: It doesn't matter which side of the bread you butter—you're going to eat both sides anyway.

PROSE   POETRY

October

ON OCTOBER 1, 1908, Henry Ford introduced his famous Model T Ford car: "Few inventions have had a more profound social effect on American life than the Model T. The motel, the roadside hamburger stand, the consolidated country schoolhouse—all grew up with the Model T. . . . As roads were improved, Ford owners thought nothing of travelling half across the continent. Florida became a kind of winter Coney Island for the North. There were hundreds of jokes about the old 'Lizzie,' and her drivers, but somehow, indestructible Lizzie doggedly went through the mud and the sand. . . ." Editorial in *The New York Times* on the fiftieth anniversary of the founding of the Ford Motor Company.

Postal Special Delivery assures that your mail will have a nice leisurely journey.

On October 1, 1847, astronomer Maria Mitchell discovered a new comet, which won her a gold medal from the King of Denmark and a copper medal from the Republic of San Marino.

Politics has an image problem—recently they took a popularity poll of the Democrats and Republicans, and nobody won.

On October 1, 1871, United States troops were dispatched to Salt Lake City, Utah, to arrest Brigham Young for lewdly cohabiting with sixteen women.

Peter's Law of Social Reciprocity: If you don't go to other's funerals, how can you expect them to come to yours?

OCTOBER 2 HAS BEEN celebrated as Old Man's Day in Broughing, Hertfordshire, England, for hundreds of years. The tradition began when Matthew Wall, a wealthy sixteenth-century farmer, died. On the way to the burial, his coffin was dropped. Wall revived and knocked on the coffin lid to be let out. It is the custom to ring the church bells at first as though for a funeral and then as for a joyous occasion.

War makes human life cheap and everything else expensive.

Fortunately the wheel was invented before the automobile, otherwise the scraping noise along our highways would be unbearable.

Garage sales give me psychological support—it's reassuring to know others are stuck with the same junk I am.

On October 2, 1882, William H. Vanderbilt, the railroad tycoon, gave newspaper reporters headline material when asked whether he operated his railroads for the public benefit. Mr. Vanderbilt replied, "The public be damned! What does the public care for the railroads except to get as much out of them for as little consideration as possible!" His words were quoted all over the United States the next day.

Peter's Third-World Principle: Foreign aid is the taxing of poor people in rich countries for the benefit of rich people in poor countries.

THANKSGIVING PROCLAMATION DAY

ON OCTOBER 3, 1789, President George Washington proclaimed that the first national Thanksgiving Day was to be observed on November 26. On October 3, 1863, President Abraham Lincoln designated the last Thursday in November as Thanksgiving.

There is one sure way to abolish war forever—have World War III.

One boon to the legal profession is that you can't take it with you.

When the United States federal income tax was signed into law on October 3, 1913, a senator speaking in opposition stated, "If we allow this one percent foot in the door, at some future date it might rise to five percent!"

On October 3, 1917, Congress doubled the income-tax rates in effect during 1916.

Peter's Accident-Prevention Principle: Presence of mind is useful, but absence of body is better.

ON OCTOBER 4, 1957, the space age began as the USSR orbited Sputnik around the earth. It was the first man-made earth satellite. Weighing 185 pounds, it was fired from orbit from the USSR's Tyuratem launch site. It transmitted radio signals for 21 days.

I'm an indoors person—just because I love Mother Nature doesn't mean I want to move in with her.

On October 4, 1918, New York's Delmonico's Restaurant closed permanently. It had been the city's most famous eating place and the favorite of celebrities internationally. At its peak it had 200 chefs and waiters.

The time you enjoy wasting is not wasted.

On October 4, 1931, the first "Dick Tracy" comic strip was published by the *New York News*.

Peter's Dictum: Spend your time on trivia—you know more about trivia than you know about important matters.

On October 5, 1921, baseball fans for the first time could listen to radio broadcasts of the World Series. Those who could not attend the series heard an on-the-scene description of the plays by the sportswriter Grantland Rice.

The quizzical expression of the ape in the zoo is because he wonders whether he's his brother's keeper or his keeper's brother.

On October 5, 1892, the famous Dalton Gang held up two banks simultaneously, an action that resulted in the deaths of four bandits and four citizens in Coffeyville, Kansas.

There is nothing like having a baby to remind you that it's a changing world.

On October 5, 1854, the first baby show was held in Springfield, Ohio, with 127 babies entered.

Peter's Game Plan: It's not whether you win or lose but how much it costs to get into the game.

PICTURE MOVE
AND TALK DAY

ON OCTOBER 6, 1889, Thomas A. Edison showed his first motion picture at West Orange, New Jersey. On October 6, 1927, *The Jazz Singer*, the first feature motion picture using the new sound track, starring Al Jolson, was premiered in New York City. Actually, there were only 291 spoken words in the Warner Bros. movie, but it was the beginning of the new era in films. Jolson sang, but captions were still used for much of the story.

Baldness proves that you can come out on top and still be a loser.

On October 6, 1857, the first major chess tournament to be held in the United States took place in New York.

When his cabinet voted no on emancipation, Lincoln raised his right hand and said, "They ayes have it."

On October 6, 1917, an editor of *Literary Digest* wrote: "A strange word has gained widespread use in the ranks of our producers of popular music. It is 'jazz,' used mainly as an adjective descriptive of a band. The group that plays for dancing . . . . seems infected with the virus that they try to instil as a stimulus in others. They shake and jump and writhe in ways to suggest a return to the medieval jumping mania."

Peter's Credit-Card Principle: Even if you are out of cash you can charge straight ahead.

ON OCTOBER 7, 1942, during World War II when Denmark was under Nazi occupation, the Germans demanded anti-Semitic legislation, including requiring Jews to wear the Star of David as identification. King Christian X of Denmark attended a service in a Copenhagen synagogue and told the congregation, "If the Jews are to wear the Star of David, then we shall all wear it. You are all Danes. You are all my people."

The wheels of progress are turned by cranks.

On October 7, 1916, the most staggering intercollegiate football defeat in history took place at Atlanta, Georgia, as Georgia Tech beat Cumberland University 222–0.

A professional writer works harder than any other lazy person in the world.

October 7 is the USSR Constitution Day, a public holiday with concerts and special programs of multinational Soviet art.

Peter's Logical Rule: Men and nations tend to act rationally—when all other possibilities have been exhausted.

ON OCTOBER 8, 1904, the first automobile race for the Vanderbilt Cup started at Hicksville, Long Island, over a 30-mile course. Included among the entries: 5 Mercedeses, 3 Panhards, 2 Fiats, 2 Popes, 1 Renault, 1 Packard, 1 Simplex. The winner was George Heath, driving a Panhard.

It is better to retire too soon than too late.

On October 8, 1871, the Great Fire of Chicago began. According to legend, the fire started when Mrs. O'Leary's cow kicked over a lantern in the barn.

If there were no such thing as tennis, cardiologists would have had to invent it.

On October 8, 1956, in the fifth game of the World Series in New York, Don Larsen of the New York Yankees pitched a perfect game against the Brooklyn Dodgers, winning 2–0. Larsen did not yield a hit or a run, or pass a batsman. No Brooklyn player reached first base. This was the first no-hitter in the history of the World Series.

Peter's Boating Principle: People waste time, effort, and money on all kinds of things that don't make sense—when by owning a boat one can consolidate and waste them all on one thing.

By PRESIDENTIAL PROCLAMATION, since 1964, Leif Ericson Day is always October 9. It honors the Norwegian explorer Leif Ericson, who discovered Vinland (North America) on October 9, 1000. Some historians believe that he landed in the area of New England.

Sex is the only game that is never called off on account of darkness.

Memory is what makes you wonder what you have forgotten.

Middle age is when you can do just as much as you could ever do—but would rather not.

October 9 is Universal Postal Union Day, an international day observed by the organization of the United Nations.

Peter's Bureaucratic Postulate: Massive expenditures obscure the evidence of bad judgment.

ON OCTOBER 10, 1886, a tailless dress coat for men, introduced from England, was worn for the first time in the United States at the Tuxedo Club, New York. The coat was worn by a club member, Griswold Lorillard. Most of the guests at the club that evening were shocked at such informality, but the "tuxedo" eventually became more commonplace in the United States than the tailcoat.

The best way to win an argument is to begin by being right.

If a cluttered desk is a sign of a cluttered mind, what's the significance of a clean desk?

Modesty is the practice of withholding from others the high opinion you hold of yourself.

On October 10, 1870, John Wesley Hyatt won a $10,000 prize by producing the best substitute for an ivory billiard ball—Celluloid. This was the beginning of the plastics industry.

Peter's Nostalgia Principle: One shouldn't live in the past—even though the price is right.

ELEANOR ROOSEVELT'S BIRTHDAY

(ANNA) ELEANOR ROOSEVELT, wife of President Franklin D. Roosevelt, was born in New York City on October 11, 1884. She attended school in England and after her marriage was her husband's partner in his political career. She raised five children and at the same time provided help and inspiration for her husband in his struggle with the crippling effects of polio. She was active in the Women's Trade Union League, the Democratic party, and state and national political campaigns. She instituted regular White House press conferences for women correspondents. She conducted a regular fifteen-minute radio commentary. In 1936, she began a daily syndicated newspaper column, "My Day." She supported and initiated many humanitarian projects, and after her husband's death was appointed a delegate to the United Nations. President John F. Kennedy called her "one of the great ladies in the history of this country." In countless polls, both national and international, she was selected as the world's most admired woman.

A duck is a bird that walks as though it had been riding a horse all day.

On October 11, 1936, *Professor Quiz*, the first "quiz" program on radio to attract national attention, started its longtime run over the facilities of the Columbia Broadcasting System.

Peter's Basic Assumption: Reality is a hypothesis.

COLUMBUS DAY (TRADITIONAL)

October 12

ON OCTOBER 12, 1492, at two o'clock in the morning, Roderigo de Triana, a sailor aboard the Pinta, one of the three vessels in the expedition led by Christopher Columbus, sighted land. Landing, Columbus took possession in the name of Ferdinand and Isabella of Spain. This landing probably took place on the east coast of the Bahamas in the vicinity of the present San Salvador (Watling) Island. By Presidential Proclamation, Columbus Day is now observed in the United States on the second Monday in October.

One of the hardest things to tolerate is a braggart who makes good.

On October 12, 1920, construction of the Holland Tunnel began. The twin tunnels under the Hudson River connect New York City with Jersey City, New Jersey.

A fatal collision can ruin your whole day.

On October 12, 1915, Edith Cavell, heroic English nurse, was executed by a German firing squad after admitting she had assisted 200 English, French, and Belgian patriots to gain their freedom from occupied Belgium.

Peter's Etiquette Principle: At a formal dinner, chewing on a steak bone is bad taste that tastes good.

ON OCTOBER 13, 1792, George Washington laid the cornerstone of the Executive Mansion, the first public building to be constructed in Washington. It was designed by James Hoban as a replica of the Duke of Leinster's Palace in Ireland. It won for its architect a $500 prize in a competition. The mansion was burned by the British in 1814 and restored in 1818. The stones were painted white to cover the marks of the fire. From that restoration it was given the name White House.

The H-bombs are being made smaller and smaller—and I can't wait for them to reach the vanishing point.

The trouble with old age is there is not much future in it.

Ignorance of one's ignorance is the greatest ignorance.

On October 13, 1962, drama critics and the audience applauded the opening in New York of Edward Albee's first full-length play, *Who's Afraid of Virginia Woolf?*

Peter's Cogent Law: Efficiency is a highly developed form of laziness.

ON OCTOBER 14, 1912, former President Theodore Roosevelt, campaigning for a third term, was shot by a would-be assassin in Milwaukee. Roosevelt refused to have his breast wound treated at a hospital until he spoke at a scheduled political rally, saying, "It may be the last speech I deliver, but I am going to deliver this one." He was treated at a local hospital after he made his speech, and then he insisted on completing his trip to Chicago.

A really educated person is one who reads the newest books on science and the oldest books of literature.

On October 14, 1930, Ethel Merman brought down the house when she held a high C for 16 bars during her rendition of "I Got Rhythm" in George Gershwin's musical, *Girl Crazy*.

Money makes the candidate go round.

On October 14, 1947, U.S. Air Force Captain Charles E. Yeager made the first flight faster than the speed of sound.

Peter's Mathematical Principle: Even though they may appear similar, learning to subtract is less important than learning to deduct.

ON OCTOBER 15, 1764, Edward Gibbon was inspired to write his great work, *The Decline and Fall of the Roman Empire,* while the barefooted friars were singing vespers in the Temple of Jupiter in Rome. Twenty-four years and six volumes later, he had completed the writing.

A bore is one who runs out of listeners faster than he runs out of talk.

Originality is the fine art of remembering what you hear but forgetting where you heard it.

The past is a pleasant place to visit but I wouldn't want to live there.

October 15 is also National Grouch Day.

Peter's Mental Principle: A brain is as strong as its weakest think.

ON OCTOBER 16, 1846, the first public operation with the patient under ether anesthesia was performed at Massachusetts General Hospital in Boston. The operation was performed by Dr. John C. Warren and the ether administered by Dr. William T. Morton, a dentist. Many Boston physicians looked on from the gallery. When the operation was completed, Dr. Warren told the physicians, many of whom were skeptical about the value of ether, "Gentlemen, this is no humbug!"

A budget is a financial schedule to prevent some of the month from being left over at the end of your money.

October 16 is also World Food Day, an annual observance to heighten public awareness of world food problems and the struggle against hunger, malnutrition, and poverty.

My neighbor says he's tired of hearing about the nuclear bomb— but I hope the subject will never be dropped.

On October 16, 1916, the first public birth-control clinic opened in Brooklyn, New York.

Peter's Happiness Rules: (1) Something to do, (2) Someone to love, and (3) Something to hope for.

ON OCTOBER 17, 1777, the British General John Burgoyne surrendered his forces to the Americans at Saratoga, New York, one of the great turning points of the American Revolution. Perhaps the most significant result of the American victory at Saratoga was that it assured the colonials of French assistance.

A bureaucrat is a politician who has swapped his bunk for a berth.

On October 17, 1931, America's most famous racketeer, Al Capone, was convicted of income-tax evasion by a federal court in Chicago.

America is where you can be born in a plain cabin and die in a cabin plane.

October 17, 1824, is Four Prunes Day, the day when the boardinghouse keepers in New York banded together because of the high cost of living and voted to serve boarders only four prunes each at breakfast.

Peter's Interaction Principle: A conversation does not consist of talking and listening—it consists of talking and waiting.

ON OCTOBER 18, 1869, Alaska was transferred from Russia to the United States in an official ceremony on Sitka's Castle Hill. The Russian flag was lowered in front of the governor's residence and the flag of the United States raised in its place and General Lovell H. Rousseau took formal possession of the territory for the United States.

Preoccupation with detail is the ultimate denial.

On October 18, 1892, the first commercial long-distance telephone line was officially opened between Chicago and New York.

What four out of five doctors recommend is another doctor.

On October 18, 1767, the Mason-Dixon Line was established as the border between Maryland and Pennsylvania. The line was based on the computations of two English surveyors, Charles Mason and Jeremiah Dixon. Everything north of the line came to be known as the North and everything south as the South.

Peter's Metric Plan: We should go metric every inch of the way.

ON OCTOBER 19, 1860, Abraham Lincoln responded to an 11-year-old girl, Grace Bedell, who had written to him on October 15, saying that she would try to persuade her four brothers to vote for him for President if he grew a beard. He wrote, "My dear little Miss . . . As to the whiskers, having never worn any, do you not think people would call it a piece of silly affectation if I were to begin it now?" By November 26, 1860, soon after he won the election, a newspaper portrait showed Lincoln with the beginnings of his beard.

The safety rule for avoiding burning your hands in hot water is to feel the water before putting your hands in it.

On October 19, 1744, the Earl of Sandwich, creator of the sandwich, said in London, "Sandwiches should be eaten with a civilized swallow not a barbarous bolt."

Even when treading the paths of righteousness use reasonable care.

Yorktown Day commemorates the surrender of Lord Cornwallis at Yorktown, Virginia, on October 19, 1781, an event that ended the American Revolutionary War.

Peter's Theory of Forecasting: All predictions are unreliable, particularly those about the future.

OCTOBER 20, 1973, was the dramatic turning point in the historically significant Watergate Affair. During the swiftly moving events of Saturday, October 20, the White House announced at 8:24 P.M., (EDT) that President Richard M. Nixon had fired Archibald Cox, Special Watergate Prosecutor, and William D. Ruckelshaus, Deputy Attorney General. Attorney General Elliott L. Richardson resigned. Public and governmental response was immediate and widespread for impeachment of the President and these demands were not quieted until President Nixon resigned on August 9, 1974.

In the stock market, fools rush in where wise men fear to trade.

The civil service is not the place to seek civility of service.

He isn't really a liar—he just recalls things that never happened.

On October 20, 1873, P. T. Barnum opened the Hippodrome in New York City to accommodate his "Greatest Show on Earth."

Peter's Educational Motto: Help fight truth decay.

ELECTRIC INCANDESCENT LAMP ANNIVERSARY

OCTOBER 21 is the anniversary of the invention in 1879 of the first practical electric incandescent lamp. After 14 months of experimentation at his Menlo Park, New Jersey, laboratory, Thomas Alva Edison achieved a workable electric lamp. He said, "The longer it burned, the more fascinated we were. . . . There was no sleep for any of us for 40 hours."

If you are too busy to laugh—you are too busy.

The great slag-heap avalanche occurred in Aberfan, Wales, October 21, 1966.

I can take all things philosophically—as long as they don't concern me.

October 21 is the Battle of Trafalgar Anniversary. On this day in 1805, the British fleet under Horatio Nelson met the combined fleets of Spain and France. Four hours later the British emerged victorious but Nelson was dead.

Peter's Assembly Principle: If it goes together easily, you're doing it wrong.

PARACHUTE FALL-OUT DAY   *October 22*

ON OCTOBER 22, 1797, André Jacques Garnerin executed the first successful parachute jump from a balloon at Monceau Park in Paris. He managed to achieve an altitude of 3,000 feet and then released his 30-foot-wide parachute from the balloon. During his descent Garnerin swung back and forth like a pendulum, which caused him to become violently ill on some of the spectators gathered on the ground beneath him.

In dieting the best way to watch calories is from a distance.

In 1670 the Virginia Assembly made it illegal for blacks to own whites for servants.

What troubles the poor is the money they can't get, and what troubles the rich is the money they can't keep.

On October 22, 1883, the first Metropolitan Opera House opened in New York City.

Peter's Theory of Political Success: Provide unintelligible answers to insoluble problems.

ON OCTOBER 23, 1910, at Fort Wayne, Indiana, Blanche S. Scott became the first woman to make a public airplane flight by herself. Miss Scott rose to a height of 12 feet, a thrilling performance for 1910.

An assumption is the first step toward a goof-up.

You can flatter anyone by telling him that he is the kind of person who can't be flattered.

Have the courage to stand up and say what I think.

October 23 is the traditional date for the swallows to depart for the winter from the old mission of San Juan Capistrano, California.

Peter's Sportsmanship Principle: It's not important whether you win or lose but how you place the blame.

UNITED NATIONS DAY commemorates founding of the United Nations and the day the charter became effective, October 24, 1945. In the United States, United Nations Day is observed by Presidential Proclamation.

Never judge presidential timber by its bark.

On October 24, 1901, in a stunt to raise money to repay a loan, Mrs. Anna Edson Taylor became the first person to survive going over Niagara Falls in a barrel. The barrel was equipped with a harness and padding, leading one reporter to say that Mrs. Taylor "seems to be taking a lot of credit that belongs to the barrel."

Prejudice is a laborsaving device that enables you to form opinions without having to dig up the facts.

On October 25, 1694, Admiral Edward Russell gave a grand entertainment at Alicante, Spain. Its most unique feature was the use of a huge marble fountain in the garden as a punch bowl. The punch contained 4 hogsheads of brandy, 126 gallons of Malaga wine, 20 gallons of lime juice, 2,500 lemons, 1,300 pounds of sugar, and 5 pounds of grated nutmeg.

Peter's Critical Principle: The way we find fault, you'd think there was a reward.

SAINT CRISPIN AND HIS BROTHER were Roman Christians who were martyred on October 25, 287. They preached during the day and made shoes at night for a living and thus became the patron saints of shoemakers. This is the prayer offered to Saint Crispin.

> Dear Saint, the saint of those who make good shoes,
> Thee for my patron saint I also choose.
> Whene'er I walk in highway, trail or street,
> Bring thou unblistered home my grateful feet.

Those who are against capital punishment have never tried it.

Mid-life is when you know where it's at, but it's farther than you care to go.

The worst thing about a bore is not that he won't stop talking— but that he won't let you stop listening.

The Charge of the Light Brigade occurred on October 25, 1854, during the Crimean War. Some 670 men of the English light cavalry brigade charged a heavily protected Russian post. The Russians killed or wounded two-thirds of the entire force. The charge was the inspiration for Alfred Lord Tennyson's heroic poem.

Peter's Positive Principle: If you are attempting the impossible— you will fail.

ON OCTOBER 26, 1825, the Erie Canal, the first of the great man-made waterways of the United States, was opened. As the highlight of the opening of the canal, which extends from Buffalo to Albany, New York, and connects Lake Erie with the Hudson River, Governor De Witt Clinton and a party of state officials boarded the canal boat *Seneca Chief* and set out for a trip to New York City. They arrived there November 4 after witnessing town and village celebrations all along the route.

It's not difficult for a woman to combine a family and a career—if she knows how to put both of them first.

Nothing is certain but death and higher taxes.

I'd like to be a pessimist, but it wouldn't work out.

On October 26, 1369, Charles V, king of France, dedicated a monument to his personal chef, Bankels, who had created a recipe for pickled fish that was favored by His Majesty. The king was called, "Charles the Wise."

Peter's Principle of Government: Everything it touches turns to mold.

OCTOBER 27, GOOD BEAR DAY, is sponsored by an organization called Good Bears of the World. The organization promotes humanitarian treatment of the young, and establishment of better understanding and love for all children. Good Bear Day honors the memory of President Theodore (Teddy) Roosevelt, born October 27, 1838, for whom the Teddy Bear was named.

A family budget is a detailed record of how you spent more than you earned.

On October 27, 1871, William Marcy (Boss) Tweed, the corrupt New York political leader of Tammany Hall, was arrested on charges of defrauding the city of millions of dollars.

The meek shall inherit the earth—when they become more aggressive about having it.

On October 27, 1904, the New York subway opened. It ran from the Brooklyn Bridge to midtown Manhattan.

Peter's Group-Action Principle: Committees agree on actions that as individuals they know are silly.

THE TOLERANTS SPONSOR this day to commemorate the birth of Erasmus, October 28, 1466, author of *In Praise of Folly*, which pokes fun at the stuffed shirts of his day. Celebrate Folly Day by making fun of all today's self-important stuffed shirts.

Living well is the best revenge.

October 28, 1977, was the first Mother-in-Law Day, a time to honor Mothers-in-Law for their contributions to families and for their good humor in suffering all the bad jokes about them. Mother-in-Law Day is now observed the third Sunday of October.

The difference between a prejudice and a conviction is that you can explain a conviction without getting mad.

On October 28, 1919, the Volstead Prohibition Enforcement Act was passed. It ruled that any beverage containing 0.5 percent alcohol was intoxicating.

Peter's Silent Principle: Saying nothing indicates a fine command of the English language.

ON OCTOBER 29, 1636, Henry Wilby, known as the Grub Street Hermit, died at 84 years of age. For the last 44 years of his life he had lived in seclusion without seeing anyone except an aged, single maidservant. Until he was 40, he was a prosperous country gentleman of Lincolnshire, but a duel fought with his brother disenchanted him with the world and he retreated from it entirely. Day in and day out, for 44 years, his main food was oatmeal, and although his life may have lacked excitement, it was apparently a healthy and long life.

In prosperity, prepare for change—in adversity, hope for it.

Two people can live as cheaply as one what?

In Hollywood it's not who you know—it's who you yes.

On October 29, 1929, the New York stock market crashed. The day went down in history as Black Tuesday. This was four days after President Herbert Hoover had declared, "The fundamental business of this country . . . is on a sound and prosperous basis." The nation faced the decade of the Great Depression.

Peter's Stoned Principle: Reality is for people who can't face drugs.

ON OCTOBER 30, 1938, Orson Welles caused a national panic when he produced over the Columbia Broadcasting System a radio dramatization of H. G. Wells's *The War of the Worlds*. Simulating typical news broadcasts of the day, the program was interrupted regularly by "bulletins" describing the invasion of New Jersey by men from Mars. Even though a clear explanation of the program had preceded the broadcast, thousands of radio listeners rushed out of their homes, many of them setting out for remote spots in the country. Hysterical people tied up the telephone lines, and police stations and hospitals were besieged by terror-stricken crowds.

Pick a winner—anyone can pick a loser.

On October 30, 1940, Franklin D. Roosevelt said, "I shall say it again and again. Your boys are not going to be sent into any foreign wars."

The history of science is the only history that shows cumulative progress of knowledge; therefore science is the only yardstick by which we can measure the progress of mankind.

On October 30, 1929, heavy selling followed the first day after the crash of October 29 on the New York Stock Exchange. John D. Rockefeller and Son announced that they were buying "sound common stocks" for investment, in the hope this would restore confidence in the market, but they were unable to stem the decline.

Peter's Fair-Play Principle: All I want is a fair advantage.

ON OCTOBER 31 in ancient England the Druids celebrated "Summer's End" with human sacrifice, forecasts, and prayers. Spirits were thought to be about as the sun began its downward course. Later it became Hallow E'en, still with ghosts, goblins, and divinations, but with much gaiety and hijinks. Apples played a major role in Halloween festivities with apple-bobbing or ducking for apples being popular pastimes. The Halloween fire and fireworks came from a custom in Lancashire where country people tried to help the souls of friends in purgatory by lighting fires and throwing on masses of burning straw with pitchforks.

For the Halloween party, my son disguised himself as a dump truck and got loaded.

Psychiatry is a way of solving our problems through confessing our parents' shortcomings.

Before television talk shows, authors had to make their reputations by writing.

October 31 is National Magic Day, observed on the anniversary of the death of magician Harry Houdini in 1926.

Peter's Survival Principle: Lead, follow, or get out of the way.

November

Freedom implies the right to make choices, but we are not free to choose to break the laws of the land. Penalties are imposed if we make that choice. We have freedom to be creative and fulfill our unique individuality, but we do not have freedom to impose our will on our environment in violation of natural laws. The penalty for violation of the environment is often paid for later by the innocent bystander, rather than by the perpetrator of the crime. This means, unfortunately, that the natural penalty need not deter the offender.

LAURENCE J. PETER,
from *The Peter Plan*

ON NOVEMBER 1, 1939, a rabbit produced by artificial insemination was exhibited at the New York Academy of Medicine. The bunny didn't know why it was such a celebrity (or who its father was). On November 1, 1944, an invisible rabbit charmed the opening-night audience at the play *Harvey* in New York. Harvey also charmed the Pulitzer Awards committee. In 1945 the play by Mary Chase won the Pulitzer Drama Award.

The federal budget is like packaged bacon—a little meat on top and a lot of fat hidden underneath.

On November 1-4 the Will Rogers Birthday Celebration in Claremore, Oklahoma, honors the memory of the great American humorist.

A philosopher looking for absolute truth is like a blind man in a dark room looking for a black cat that isn't there.

On November 1, 1870, the U.S. Weather Bureau made its first weather observations.

Peter's Theory of Self: You can never really get away—you can only take yourself somewhere else.

TRUMAN BEATS THE POLLSTERS DAY

November 2

ON NOVEMBER 2, 1948, President Harry S Truman confounded the pollsters when the Truman-Barkley ticket captured 303 electoral votes and 28 states, while the Dewey-Warren ticket won 189 electoral votes and 16 states. On November 1 most political pollsters and commentators agreed that Governor Thomas E. Dewey, Republican of New York, would defeat Truman by a landslide. The experts had predicted that Dewey would carry 22 to 29 states and Truman 9 to 11 states. Truman remained calm and said that the polls were highly inaccurate.

Civilization will begin when the power of love overtakes the love of power.

All science is concerned with cause and effect. Each scientific discovery increases our ability to predict the consequences of our actions and thus our ability to control future events.

Economics is the art of trying to satisfy infinite needs with limited resources.

On November 2, 1917, the Balfour Declaration stated that "His Majesty's Government views with favour the establishment of a national home for the Jewish people in Palestine."

Peter's Medical Principle: If you are feeling well, medical care will help you get over it.

THIS DAY RECOGNIZES the inventor of the sandwich, John Montague, Fourth Earl of Sandwich, who was born November 3, 1718. England's First Lord of the Admiralty, the man after whom Captain Cook named the Sandwich Islands, was a rake and a gambler. He is said to have invented the sandwich as a timesaving snack to be eaten while he was engaged in 24-hour-long gambling sessions.

A team of mountain climbers rope themselves together to prevent the sensible ones from going home.

My wife has two complaints: she has nothing to wear and she doesn't have enough closet space.

It is good sportsmanship not to pick up lost golf balls while they are still rolling.

On November 3, 1837, Illinois housewives were irate over the cost of living. A pound of butter could cost as much as 8 cents, a dozen eggs 6 cents, beef was 3 cents a pound, pork 2 cents, coffee was 20 cents a pound, and sugar was 10 cents a pound.

Peter's Avoidance-of-Trouble Dictum: Don't be superstitious—it brings bad luck.

THE NO BULL PEACE PRIZE is sponsored by Dr. Laurence J. Peter and presented by the "Peter University" for significant contributions to the cause of world peace. The prize is presented to an individual, or individuals, who voluntarily, not because of job or political position, work for peace. The prize is presented on the anniversary of Will Rogers's Birthday, November 4, 1879, in commemoration of his many humanitarian endeavors and his contributions to international understanding.

In the steadfast search for peace, man has always stuck to his guns.

What we crave is the peace that passeth all misunderstanding.

The dove of peace is a bird of paradise.

Although artifical legs had been built previously, on November 4, 1846, Benjamin F. Palmer of Meredith, New Hampshire, produced a leg with a significant new feature—a practical joint that moved noiselessly.

Peter's Mental-Health Rule: Never sleep with anyone crazier than yourself.

ON NOVEMBER 5, 1605, Guy Fawkes was arrested at the entrance to a vault beneath the old House of Lords in London. He had a darkened lantern, a tinder box, and three matches in his possession and was making preparations for the following day to light the fuse to 36 barrels of gunpowder that he and his coconspirators had placed there. With his arrest the famous Gunpowder Plot to take the lives of King James I and the assembled Parliament came to an end. If the plot had succeeded, a Catholic monarchy would have been installed and the course of history would have been changed. Guy Fawkes Day, an important day in British history, is unusual in that it commemorates a man for what he failed to do.

The cold war allows the world neither to live in peace nor to rest in peace.

November 5 is World Community Day, an annual celebration since 1943 that focuses on global justice and peace.

The cold war will come to an end when each side is ahead of the other in the arms race.

On November 5, 1895, George B. Selden of Rochester, New York, was granted the first United States automobile patent for which he had applied in 1879. Although his patent covered every essential feature of the modern automobile, he received only $200,000 when he sold his rights in 1899.

Peter's Negative-Outcome Rule: Whenever you get a mouthful of too-hot soup, the next thing you do will be wrong.

ON NOVEMBER 6, 1940, to show the world that the United States were united despite the partisan sentiments expressed all during the presidential campaign that ended on November 5 with the reelection of President Franklin D. Roosevelt, 3,000 people staged a United American Rally at Carnegie Hall in New York. The promoters of this rally wanted to make it clear to the Axis powers in Europe that the majority of Democrats and Republicans in this country shared a mutual abhorrence of Fascism.

I will do almost anything to get a laugh as long as I don't have to resort to good taste.

On November 6, 1962, after defeat in his campaign for governor of California, Richard M. Nixon told the press, "You won't have Dick Nixon to kick around anymore."

A few reels of our last trip soon put our guests in a traveling mood.

On November 6, 1869, the first intercollegiate football game was played by Princeton and Rutgers. Rutgers won 6–4.

Peter's Advertising Principle: The only person you can be sure will read a sign is the one who paid for it.

SEA-TO-SHINING-SEA ANNIVERSARY

ON NOVEMBER 7, 1805, Lewis and Clark sighted the Pacific Ocean for the first time at the mouth of the Columbia River in the "Oregon Country," thus proving that America was a vast continent stretching between two oceans. One of the great explorations in American history, the Lewis and Clark Expedition was authorized by President Jefferson as a fact-finding mission about the vast tract of land purchased from France in 1803, the so-called Louisiana Purchase. Congress appropriated $2,500 to defray the expenses of Lewis and Clark during their travels.

Communism is a system of government under which it is impossible to lose an election bet.

On November 7, 1874, *Harper's Weekly* published the first cartoon depicting an elephant as the symbol of the Republican Party in America.

A synonym is the word to use when you can't spell the right one, and therefore can't even find it in the dictionary.

On November 7, 1916, Jeannette Rankin of Montana became the first woman to be elected to the U.S. House of Representatives.

Peter's Bureaucratic Rule: Ask an intelligent question; receive the eternal runaround.

NOVEMBER 8 IS SPONSORED by Punsters Unlimited as a time to compose an incredibly dreadful pun to bore and PUNish your friends with it.

A friend once asked Ben Jonson to make a pun. He replied, "What subject?" His friend responded, "The king." "But," said Jonson, "the king is not a subject. He is king."

The greatest American composer is the tranquilizer.

November 8 is Dunce Day in memory of Duns Scotus, the medieval scholar whose concern with minuscule technicalities brought the word *dunce* into the language. Honor the day by not overemphasizing the picayune, by not being a dunce.

All the world's a stage, and most of us are stagehands.

On November 8, 1793, the Louvre, the great Paris museum of art, was opened to the public.

Peter's Famous Rule: If you have to tell people you're famous— you're not.

TWENTIETH CENTURY TECHNOLOGICAL VULNERABILITY DAY

ON NOVEMBER 9, 1965, the East Coast Blackout caused by a massive electrical power failure started in western New York State at 5:17 P.M. It cut electrical power to much of the northeastern United States and to Ontario and Quebec in Canada. Over 30 million persons and 80,000 square miles were affected for from two to thirteen hours. This experience provoked a number of studies of the vulnerability of twentieth century societal technology and of what people do in the dark.

The art of compromise is the ability to cut the cake so that each thinks he is getting the biggest piece.

Modern youth are a lot alike in many disrespects.

Watermelon is food, drink, and entertainment—with it you can eat the flesh, drink the juice, wash your face, and play with the seeds.

On November 9, 1906, Theodore Roosevelt became the first President to leave the United States while in office when he sailed to the Panama Canal Zone.

Peter's Theory of Prediction: The future will be very much like the present, only longer.

ONE OF THE MOST publicized meetings of all time occurred on November 10, 1871, when Henry M. Stanley, a newspaperman and explorer, discovered the missing Scottish missionary and explorer, David Livingstone, in a small settlement in "darkest Africa." Coming face to face with the missing man in Ujiji, Central Africa, Stanley said, "Dr. Livingstone, I presume?" And Livingstone answered: "Yes and I feel thankful that I am here to welcome you." Livingstone was seeking to trace the source of the river Nile. He continued his exploration until the year of his death in 1873.

Computer intelligence will never replace the human mind until it is able to blame its mistakes on other computers.

On November 10, 1888, a 13-year-old concert violinist, Fritz Kreisler, made his American debut at Steinway Hall in New York.

By the time you catch up with the Joneses, they start refinancing.

On November 10, 1933, Adolf Hitler said, "I am insulted by the repeated assertion that I want war. Am I a fool? War! It would settle nothing."

Peter's Ascendancy Rule: Whatever goes up will go up more after the first of the month.

VETERANS DAY   *November 11*

VETERANS DAY BEGAN as Armistice Day, the cessation of hostilities ending World War I at 11:00 A.M., November 11, 1918. The anniversary of the day is celebrated in various places as Armistice Day, Remembrance Day, Victory Day, World War I Memorial Day, and Veterans Day. Many places observe a silent memorial at the eleventh hour of the eleventh day of the eleventh month of each year. By Presidential Proclamation, since 1954 the name has been changed from Armistice to Veterans Day. A further Presidential Proclamation required that beginning in 1971 it would be observed each year on the fourth Monday in October. This movable observance, which separated Veterans Day from Armistice Day, proved unpopular, so another Presidential Proclamation required that, effective January 1978, the observance of Veterans Day revert to November 11.

Peace is the lull between wars established to enable the generals to write their books.

Whoever said, "Where there's smoke, there's fire," never had a fireplace.

It is a fact that women live longer than men—especially widows.

On November 11, 1939, Kate Smith sang Irving Berlin's "God Bless America" on her radio program. Soon it had almost assumed the status of a national anthem. Although the song was written in 1917, the public had not heard it until it was introduced b Kate Smith.

Peter's Advice-for-Writing Principle: Try to erase the fine line between satire and boredom.

ON NOVEMBER 12, 1946, the first "autobank" was established by the Exchange National Bank of Chicago. This was the beginning of transacting your banking business without leaving your car.

Jumping to conclusions seldom leads to happy landings.

You can fall in love, but you have to climb out.

Times change—today cars are a necessity and children are luxuries.

On November 12, 1954, a bitter session over the proposed motion to censure Senator Joseph R. McCarthy (R.-Wis.) was interrupted by Senator Barry Goldwater (R.-Ariz.) who rose to the defense of McCarthy and said, in part: "The news columns and the airwaves have been filled with their pious talk about 'civil liberties,' 'ethical codes,' and 'protection of the innocent,' while at the same time these people have dipped into the smut pot to discredit Senator McCarthy and his work against Communism . . ."

Peter's Law of Emulation: When an aggressor and defender engage in conflict, they soon tend to mirror each other's behavior and character.

THE RELEASE ON NOVEMBER 13, 1921, of the moving picture *The Sheik*, starring the great lover Rudolph Valentino, was a milestone in the motion-picture industry. Women in the audience were said to have swooned when they were carried away by the masculinity of the image on the screen. Leading men in movies have tried ever since to capture the romanticism of the Italian-born hero of this picture.

Confidence is that feeling you have just before you understand the situation.

You've reached middle age when it's the doctor who tells you to slow down instead of the police.

A hamburger by any other name costs twice as much.

On November 13, 1933, the first recorded sit-down strike in the United States occurred at the Hormel Packing Company in Austin, Minnesota.

Peter's Bureaucratic-Power Principle: Whenever a bureaucracy acquires a technique that enhances its power, that technique will soon be adopted by the other bureaucracies.

ON NOVEMBER 14, 1832, the first streetcar in the world made its appearance on the streets of New York. Actually, New Yorkers referred to the new conveyance as a "horse car," because the car was drawn by two horses on tracks laid on Fourth Avenue between Prince and Fourteenth streets. A total of 30 people could be accommodated in the 3 compartments of each car.

If we want to build a new world, we should be ready—the first one was made out of chaos.

Neurotics worry about things that didn't happen in the past instead of being like normal people who worry about things that won't happen in the future.

There are two kinds of legal language—one is hard to understand and the other is easy to misunderstand.

On November 14, 1851, *Moby Dick* by Herman Melville was published in New York.

Peter's Theory of Motivation: The three primary motivators are love, power, or achievement, except for those motivated only by the love of power and achievement.

PIKES PEAK DISCOVERY DAY *November 15*

ON NOVEMBER 15, 1806, Zebulon Pike was exploring the West in an attempt to discover the source of the Mississippi River, when he sighted the mountain peak that came to be called Pikes Peak.

A major difficulty with our present situation is that all the people who know how to solve our problems are busy driving taxis and cutting hair.

On November 15, 1492, Christopher Columbus recorded the use of tobacco among the Indians, the first reference to tobacco.

Money doesn't buy happiness, but that is not the reason so many people are poor.

On November 15, 1926, the National Broadcasting Company went on the air with 24 radio stations. The inaugural four-hour broadcast was from the Grand Ballroom of the Waldorf Astoria Hotel, featuring opera stars Mary Garden and Tito Ruffa, the New York Symphony Orchestra, Will Rogers, Weber and Fields, and many others.

Peter's Social Theory: Civilization is the means of multiplying the need for nonessentials.

ON NOVEMBER 16, 1776, Statia Island, also called Saint Eustatius, one of the Caribbean Leeward Islands of the Netherlands Antilles, was the first foreign government to salute an American flag. To commemorate the anniversary of the event, festivities are held, including sports and dancing.

A child who goes to the store and forgets what his mother sent him for will most likely grow up and go to Congress.

What we want is brand-new ideas that don't upset our old ideas.

You can always identify a prejudiced person—he is the one who is too stubborn to admit you are right.

On November 16, 1933, the United States established diplomatic relations with the USSR.

Peter's First-Priority Law: If you want to be immortal, the first requirement is death.

ON NOVEMBER 17, 1869, the Suez Canal was formally opened with great pomp and circumstance. Egypt was host to 6,000 foreign guests. When the canal was declared open, a display of fireworks was ignited on each bank and a squadron of yachts passed through the canal, the first one bearing the Emperor Franz Josef of Austria-Hungary, the Empress Eugénie of France, and the khedive of Egypt.

A conservative is one who believes in moving forward in the direction of the status quo.

On November 17, 1913, Dr. Alfred C. Fones inaugurated a course for dental hygenists in Bridgeport, Connecticut. Thirty-three young women enrolled.

Yesterday I was reviewing the high points of my life and I fell asleep.

On November 17, 1800, Congress convened for its first Washington, D.C., session.

Peter's Survival Principle: The best thing to hold onto in the world is each other.

MICKEY MOUSE BIRTHDAY   *November 18*

ON NOVEMBER 18, 1928, the first animated-cartoon talking picture, *Steamboat Willie*, appeared on the screen of the Colony Theatre in New York City. The movie featured the comical antics of Mickey Mouse, using the voice of his creator, Walt Disney.

Corn is measured out West by the foot, down South by the gallon, and on television by the hour.

On November 18, 1805, 30 women met at the home of Mrs. Silas Lee in Wiscasset, Maine, to organize the Female Charitable Society. This was the first women's club in America.

One good thing about life is it's only temporary.

On November 18, 1820, U.S. Navy Captain Nathaniel B. Palmer discovered Antarctica.

Mrs. Peter's Law: Today if you are not confused, you're just not thinking clearly.

GETTYSBURG ADDRESS ANNIVERSARY

ON NOVEMBER 19, 1863, President Abraham Lincoln, at the dedication of the Gettysburg battlefield as a national cemetery, spoke for only two minutes and limited his remarks to ten sentences: ". . . we here highly resolve that these dead shall not have died in vain; that this nation, under God, shall have a new birth of freedom; and that government of the people, by the people, and for the people, shall not perish from the earth." The President's speech was considered so insignificant that most newspapers the next day carried it on inside pages in contrast to the two-hour oration delivered by Edward Everett, which was printed nationwide on page 1.

A few people with bad coughs go to the doctor, but most go to the theatre.

On November 19, 1874, William Marcy Tweed, political "boss" of Tammany Hall in New York City, was convicted of defrauding the city of about $6 million and sentenced to 12 years in prison.

There's no use worrying about life—no matter how hard you try, you'll never get out of it alive.

November 19 is the anniversary of the Jonestown Massacre. On this day in 1978 Reverend Jim Jones of the People's Temple directed the deaths of more than 900 persons at Jonestown, Guyana.

Peter's Power-of-Education Fallacy: One of our most popular illusions is that an educated, knowledgeable, and enlightened constituency will be stirred to action beyond narrow self-interest.

EFFECTIVE NOVEMBER 20, 1914, all American citizens requesting passports from the State Department were required to submit passport photographs, specially taken for this purpose, to be attached to their passports. These stark, untouched photos became a source of many jokes. "If you look like your passport photo, you're too sick to travel." "Passport photos are not for identification, but to provide laughs for foreign Customs inspectors."

Credit enables you to spend money you haven't earned, to buy things you don't need, to impress people you don't like.

On November 20, 1962, President Kennedy signed an Executive Order forbidding racial and religious discrimination in housing built or purchased with federal aid.

Life is like a shower—one wrong turn and you're in hot water.

On November 20, 1620, Peregrine White, a boy, became the first child born to English parents in New England—aboard the Mayflower the day after it arrived off Cape Cod.

Peter's Pollution-Responsibility Principle: Nuclear and toxic-chemical wastes ascend in inverse proportion to requirements that polluters take corrective action—the bigger the mess, the less the redress.

NOVEMBER 21 is sponsored by Hello Day International and everyone on earth who chooses to participate says "Hello" to ten people to whom he has never spoken before.

We have the same thing every Thanksgiving—relatives.

On November 21, 1925, Harold E. (Red) Grange, the most famous football player of his day, played his last varsity game for the University of Illinois. When he turned professional his popularity soared and he received rewarding offers for personal appearances and a movie contract. President Coolidge received him at the White House.

My wife overcooked the turkey so I bought her a book on bird watching.

On November 21, 1783, François Pilâtre de Rozier and the Marquis d'Arlandes soared to 300 feet and traveled five miles in the first manned hot-air-balloon voyage.

Peter's Historical Principle: Those who fail to study the past are bound to repeat its mistakes. Those who do study the past will goof up in new ways.

ON NOVEMBER 22, 1906, delegates to the International Radio Telegraphic Convention in Berlin, Germany, adopted SOS as the letters for the new international distress signal, particularly for ships at sea and aircraft, but also as any call for help.

Jack Sprat could eat no fat, his wife could eat no lean—he forgot his credit card.

On November 22, 1909, Miss Helen Hayes made her stage debut at the Herald Square Theatre in the play *In Old Dutch*.

Willpower is when you start your diet on Thanksgiving Day.

On November 22, 1963, President John F. Kennedy was struck down by an assassin's bullet as he rode in a motorcade in Dallas, Texas.

Peter's Immutable Law II: The unexpected always happens.

ON NOVEMBER 23, 1911, Earl Ovington was sworn in as the first airmail pilot of the U.S. Post Office. His assignment was to deliver mail handed to him by the postmaster at Garden City, Long Island, to the postmaster of Mineola six miles away. He flew a Blériot monoplane, the *Dragon Fly*, in the first U.S. Post Office-authorized airmail service.

If you can manage to stay scared all the time, you will find that the occasional crisis won't bother you one bit.

On November 23, 1896, the current issue of the *Home Maker's Magazine* said, "The barbecue is to Georgia what the clambake is to Rhode Island."

They served an Early American Thanksgiving Dinner—nothing frozen, everything came out of cans.

On November 23, 1876, at a meeting in Springfield, Massachusetts, three eastern colleges, Columbia, Princeton, and Harvard, formed the first intercollegiate football association.

Peter's Metalaw (law about laws): Where a law is not needed, it will work perfectly—where it is desperately needed, it will fail.

On November 24, 1869, women representing 21 states of the Union convened in Cleveland to draw up plans for the organization of the American Woman Suffrage Association. This broadly representative initial meeting was chaired by the vigorous Woman's Rights' leader, Lucy Stone, and the main speaker was Julia Ward Howe.

I ate so much at Thanksgiving dinner, they put me on the critical list at Weight Watchers.

On November 24, 1963, Lee Harvey Oswald, the assassin of President Kennedy, was being transferred from the Dallas police station to an armored car, in order to be driven to the county jail, when Jack Ruby pressed through the crowd and fatally shot him. The incredible features of this shooting were: (1) It was recorded by television news, and (2) Ruby had little difficulty getting close to the prisoner despite the fact that Oswald was surrounded by 60 policemen.

The meek shall inherit the earth when it's in such a condition that nobody wants it.

On November 24, 1874, Joseph F. Glidden of De Kalb, Illinois, was granted a patent for barbed wire.

Peter's Writing Principle: Authors feel that when they have stated a problem clearly, and told how it should be solved, things are somehow better.

ON NOVEMBER 25, 1973, a presidential order required a cutback in automotive speed from 70 to 55 miles per hour for highway driving, as an energy-conservation measure. In addition to the fuel saving, initially projected at 200,000 barrels a day, it is estimated that an average of 9,000 lives are saved each year as a result of the lowered speed limit.

Democracy is a process of stumbling to the right decision through freely choosing which candidate will be allowed to mess things up for us.

On November 25, 1903, Robert (Bob) Fitzsimmons won the light-heavyweight boxing championship, making him the first in history to have won world championships in three weight divisions, including the middleweight and heavyweight titles.

Thanksgiving is when millions of Americans finally do something about their weight—increase it.

On November 25, 1834, the proprietor of Delmonico's, one of New York's finest restaurants, advised the public that a meal of soup, steak, coffee, and half a pie cost 12 cents. Dinner for two could be served for 25 cents, the extra penny providing for a second cup of coffee.

Peter's Superficial Law: You only scratch the surface because there is nothing you can scratch but the surface.

ON NOVEMBER 26, 1864, a young mathematics instructor at Oxford University, England, sent an early Christmas gift to 12-year-old Alice Liddell, the daughter of a country clergyman. The gift was his handwritten manuscript of a story he had composed for Alice. The instructor was Charles L. Dodgson and he called his story *Alice's Adventures Underground*. We know the story today as *Alice's Adventures in Wonderland* and *Through the Looking-Glass* and the instructor by his pen name, Lewis Carroll. Dodgson remained a bachelor all of his life.

The shortest distance between two points is always under repair.

On November 26, 1925, many Americans considered becoming motorists when the price of the popular Ford "roadster" was announced at $260.

Early to bed and early to rise—'till you make enough money to do otherwise.

The first United States holiday by Presidential Proclamation was Thanksgiving day, November 26, 1789. Later, Abraham Lincoln issued a proclamation setting Thanksgiving as the last Thursday in November.

Peter's Inflation Principle: Money no longer talks—it just goes without saying.

ON NOVEMBER 27, 1937, members of the International Ladies' Garment Workers' Union in New York produced a musical revue entitled *Pins and Needles*, a clever and tuneful plea for organized labor. First-night spectators and critics alike were impressed by the originality of the show and particularly liked a song called "Sing Me a Song of Social Significance." The cast was made up of amateurs but the lively little revue continued until 1939.

No two people are exactly alike—and they're both glad about it.

On November 27, 1890, residents in Boston suburbs complained to police that it was unsafe to drive their horses and buggies on country lanes because of racing bicyclists.

A doctor should leave the well enough alone.

On November 27, 1889, Curtis P. Bradly received the first permit to drive an automobile through Central Park. The permit was issued by the Commissioner of Parks of New York City on the condition that Bradly pledge "to exert the greatest care to avoid frightening horses."

Peter's Longevity Principle: Although living to a ripe old age may not guarantee wealth and happiness, it beats the alternative.

ON NOVEMBER 28, 1895, America's first automobile race got under way when six cars started a 55-mile round-trip course from Chicago's Jackson Park to Evanston, Illinois. Two of the cars were electrically driven and four were powered by gasoline engines. The winner was J. Frank Duryea, who drove an automobile designed by his brother Charles E. Duryea. The winner traveled at an average speed of 7 miles per hour. The Duryea car used 3.5 gallons of gasoline and 19 gallons of water. Mr. Duryea's prize from the *Chicago Times-Herald* was $2000.

Success is complicated—you've got to deliver the goods but not get caught with them.

The first thing a child learns after he gets his first drum is that he will never get another.

When a doctor doesn't know, he calls it a virus—if he can't cure it, he calls it an allergy.

On November 28, 1520, Ferdinand Magellan began his crossing of the Pacific Ocean.

Peter's IRS Rule: The wages of sin go unreported.

KING TUT'S DISCOVERY DAY *November 29*

ON NOVEMBER 29, 1922, Lord Carnarvon of England and his American assistant, Howard Carter, discovered the tomb of King Tutankhamen in Egypt. Their accomplishment was hailed by the newspapers of the world as "the greatest archaeological discovery of all time." The average American wasn't much concerned with the archaeological importance of the mission, but was fascinated by the treasure in the tomb. To people in the United States, in 1922 and 1923, the king was known as King Tut. Recent years have seen a revival of interest in the king because of a worldwide tour of the Tutankhamen treasures.

A penny and a nickel don't have much value today, but a dime makes a good screwdriver.

On November 29, 1929, Lieutenant Commander Richard E. Byrd flew over the South Pole in his tri-motored Fokker plane. Byrd became the only person until this time to have flown over both the North and South poles.

How can a physician's fee be anything but ill-gotten gains?

On November 29, 1890, football teams of the U.S. Military Academy and the U.S. Naval Academy held the first Army-Navy game at West Point, New York. Score: Navy 25, Army 0.

Peter's Performance Principle: In jobs where performance cannot be easily measured, promotion beyond one's level of competence is accelerated.

SAINT ANDREW WAS a brother of Saint Peter and an apostle of Christ. Following the death of Jesus he was a missionary throughout the Middle East. About A.D. 60, on November 30 he was crucified on an X-shaped cross, fastened to it by cords instead of nails to produce a more lingering death.

Saint Andrew is the patron saint of Scotland. The Feast of Saint Andrew is celebrated on this day in many places in the world. An early Saint Andrew society in the United States was founded in 1749 in Philadelphia. At the 1788 feast, 45 men consumed, in addition to the food, 38 bottles of Madeira, 27 bottles of claret, 8 bottles of port, 26 bottles of porter, 2 bottles of cider, and 2 bowls of punch.

A diplomat is one who thinks twice before saying nothing.

November 30, 1835, was the birthday of Samuel Langhorne Clemens, better known as Mark Twain, author of *Tom Sawyer*, *Huckleberry Finn*, and many other works.

Old Canadian saying: Man wants but little here below—zero.

On November 30, 1900, Oscar Wilde died in Paris. One of his last remarks was a comment about the wallpaper in his room: "One of us had to go."

_____

Peter's Theory of Change: In spite of warnings, nothing much happens until the status quo becomes more painful than change.

December

ON DECEMBER 1, 1922, the first skywriting in the United States was executed by Captain Cyril Turner of the Royal Air Force. The message that he wrote was, "Hello U.S.A.," a good choice requiring no dotting of *i*'s or crossing of *t*'s.

Where there's a will, there's an inheritance tax.

On December 1, 1913, the world's first drive-in gasoline station opened for business in Pittsburgh, Pennsylvania. Until this date, motorists bought gasoline in livery stables and garages and continued to do so until the "gas station" caught on.

Show me a man who put untested Christmas lights on the top of his house and I'll show you a "Fiddler on the Roof."

On December 1, 1879, one of the greatest evenings in the history of the American theatre took place at the Fifth Avenue Theatre in New York as Arthur Sullivan conducted *H.M.S. Pinafore*, the operetta he had composed in collaboration with William S. Gilbert. The other half of the famous team of Gilbert and Sullivan portrayed a sailor in the chorus.

Peter's Prophecy: The meek shall inherit the earth, but not the oil rights.

MONROE DOCTRINE DAY   *December 2*

PRESIDENT JAMES MONROE, in his annual message to Congress, December 2, 1823, enunciated the doctrine that bears his name, which has long been hailed as a statement of United States policy: ". . . In the wars of the European powers in matters relating to themselves we have never taken any part . . . we should consider any attempt on their part to extend their system to any portion of this hemisphere as dangerous to our peace and safety . . ."

He who inherits riches shall never know the joy of toiling endlessly to pay the bills.

On December 2, 1942, a self-sustaining nuclear chain reaction was demonstrated for the first time by a group of scientists working in great secrecy below the football stadium and tennis courts at the University of Chicago.

Christmas comes a month before arriving.

On December 2, 1816, the first savings bank to operate in the United States opened for business as the Philadelphia Savings Fund Society.

Peter's Theory of Impulse Buying: At least that's one excuse for whom we elect for president.

FIRST JAZZ CONCERTO ANNIVERSARY

ON DECEMBER 3, 1925, the American composer George Gershwin performed as soloist playing his Concerto in F at a concert in Carnegie Hall, New York. It was the first public performance of the first jazz concerto for piano in musical history.

You can fool some of the people all of the time and all of the people some of the time, but you can make a damn fool of yourself any old time.

An archaeologist is a person whose career lies in ruins.

Another Christmas miracle is that everyone receives more cards than he or she sends.

On December 3, 1967, in Cape Town, South Africa, the first human heart transplant was performed by Dr. Christian Barnard on Louis Washkansky, who lived with the new heart for 18 days.

Peter's Political Principle: Politicians make strange bedfellows, but they all share the same bunk.

ON DECEMBER 4, 1867, the National Grange of Husbandry was founded in the United States. This organization of farmers, usually called simply the Grange, contributed significantly to the development of agriculture and provided a focus for much of the social life of rural America.

There are two classes of Christmas gifts—the ones you don't like and the ones you don't get.

On December 4, 1918, President Woodrow Wilson sailed for France to attend the peace conference at Versailles.

Christmas is the season when gifts are gladly given, happily received, and cheerfully refunded.

On December 4, 1933, *Tobacco Road*, a dramatization of Erskine Caldwell's novel, opened on Broadway where it ran for 3,182 performances.

Peter's Principle of Aging: Don't worry about middle age; you'll outgrow it.

PROHIBITION REPEAL DAY   *December 5*

ON DECEMBER 5, 1933, at exactly 3:32 P.M. (Mountain Time), national Prohibition came to an end when Utah, the thirtieth state, ratified the Twenty-first Amendment to the Constitution, thus repealing the Eighteenth (or Prohibition) Amendment. Eight states had voted to remain dry, but the "Noble Experiment" that went into effect in 1920 was now just a matter of controversial history.

The best things in life are for a fee.

On December 5, 1776, 50 men at the College of William and Mary in Williamsburg, Virginia, organized Phi Beta Kappa, the first scholastic fraternity in America.

I want to wish you all a very Merry Christmas—and for those who don't observe Christmas, a very Happy Hanukkah—and for those who don't observe Hanukkah, a very festive season.

On December 5, 1929, the American League of Physical Culture, the first nudist organization in America, was established. December does not appear to be the ideal time to start a nudist group, but the enterprise flourished.

Peter's Compensation Principle: What is considered "a living wage" depends on whether you pay it or get it.

SAINT NICHOLAS DAY   *December 6*

SAINT NICHOLAS, an archbishop of Myra, who died December 6, 342, was one of the most venerated saints of both eastern and western Christian churches. Saint Nicholas is the patron saint of Russia, mariners, youth, and virgins. From earliest times he has been one of the saints most often pictured and is especially noted for his charity. Santa Claus and the presentation of yuletide gifts derived from the works of Saint Nicholas.

Live as if you were going to die tomorrow, but learn as if you were going to live forever.

On December 6, 1917, a collision between two munitions ships, one Belgian and one French, in the harbor at Halifax, Nova Scotia, caused a violent explosion killing some 1,630 people and wounding 4,000 more. Twenty thousand residents of the city were left without homes.

One solution to the expense of Christmas is the Christmas Club—it's a well-thought-out plan to keep you poor from January through November so the stores can be rich in December.

On December 6, 1933, liquor stores, bars, and restaurants in America were crowded as the first legal alcoholic beverages in 13 years went on sale.

Peter Prevention Principle: A stitch in time saves embarrassment.

ONE OF THE ORIGINAL 13 colonies, Delaware, whose 2,057 square miles make it the second smallest state in the Union, was explored by Henry Hudson in 1609. The following year Samuel Argall's ship was blown in a storm into a bay he named Delaware in honor of his colony's governor, Lord De La Warr. As settlement took place, the men who became Delaware's leaders were strong nationalists who were aware of the benefits that their small state could derive from being part of a strong country. On December 7, 1787, Delaware became the first state to ratify the Constitution and thus enter the Union.

Anytime you hear someone say: "Youth is a state of mind," you can be sure that he has a lot more state of mind than he has youth.

On December 7, 1941, while Japanese envoys were negotiating with the State Department in Washington, the Japanese Air Force struck suddenly in the Pacific by bombing Pearl Harbor, the Philippines, Wake and Guam islands, and the British possession of Singapore. Simultaneously the Japanese forces invaded Thailand and Malaya.

On December 7, 1968, an overdrawn book was returned to the University of Cincinnati Library after 145 years—the fine was calculated to be $22,646.

Peter's Theory of Competence: The way to avoid mistakes is to gain experience. The way to gain experience is to make mistakes.

THE ENGLISH WINTER of 1818 was extremely mild. On December 8, the gardens in the neighborhood of Plymouth displayed the following flowers in full bloom: jonquils, narcissus, hyacinths, anemones, pinks, stock, African and French marigolds, passion flowers, and roses, along with ripe strawberries and raspberries. Fortunately today, although the weather is not always as cooperative as in 1818, flowers grown either indoors or outdoors are available all winter long.

Life is like a game of bridge—a dummy puts all his cards on the table.

On December 8, 1776, George Washington crossed the Delaware River, near Trenton, New Jersey, and landed on Pennsylvania soil.

Every year Christmas becomes less a birthday and more a clearance sale.

On December 8, 1903, Samuel P. Langley, aviation enthusiast and secretary of the Smithsonian Institution, faced his second defeat in his attempt to fly. His power-driven airplane plunged into the Potomac River.

Peter's Competence Principle: Quit while you are behind.

FIRST FORMAL
CREMATION DAY

ON DECEMBER 9, 1792, the first formal cremation of a human body in America took place near Charleston, South Carolina. Henry Laurens, colonial statesman and signer of the Treaty of Paris, ending the Revolutionary War, in his will, provided: "I do solemnly enjoin it on my son, as an indispensable duty, that as soon as he conveniently can, after my decease, he cause my body to be wrapped in twelve yards of tow cloth and burned until it be entirely consumed, and then, collecting my bones, deposit them wherever he may think proper."

This time of year I spell relief—J-U-L-Y.

On December 9, 1793, Noah Webster established *The American Minerva*, New York's first daily newspaper.

This year they're featuring the Neurotic Doll—it's already wound up.

On December 9, 1907, the first Christmas Seals were placed on sale in the Wilmington Post Office. The proceeds were devoted to the campaign against tuberculosis.

Peter's Consolation Principle: If your dreams don't come true, be thankful that neither do your nightmares.

HUMAN RIGHTS DAY   *December 10*

DECEMBER 10 is the official United Nations observance each year of Human Rights Day, the anniversary of the adoption of the "Universal Declaration of Human Rights" in 1948. The Declaration sets forth basic rights and fundamental freedoms to which all men and women everywhere in the world are entitled. In the United States a Presidential Proclamation made in 1949 identifies December 10 as Human Rights Day each year.

To be clever all you need to do is remember a phrase that nobody else has ever thought of.

On December 10, 1901, the distribution of Nobel Prizes was made for the first time on the anniversary of the death of Alfred Nobel.

Everybody is getting cynical about Christmas—the only people who believe in Santa Claus anymore are elevator operators, doormen, and janitors.

On December 10, 1950, in accepting the Nobel Prize for Literature, William Faulkner stated: "I believe that man will not merely endure: he will prevail."

Peter's Information Principle: Improvement in communication produces vastly increased areas of misunderstanding.

ON DECEMBER 11, 1929, designers of the Empire State Building in New York released this announcement: "The directors of Empire State, Incorporated, believe that in a comparatively short time the Zeppelin airships will establish transatlantic, transcontinental and transpacific lines, and possibly a route to South America from the Port of New York. Building with an eye to the future, it has been determined to erect a mooring tower atop the Empire State Building."

The person patting you on the back may only be determining where to stick the knife.

'Tis the season to be jolly—while looking for a last-minute tax shelter.

On December 11, 1946, John D. Rockefeller, Jr., announced that he had offered to donate a six-block parcel of land along the East River in New York to the United Nations as a site for its world headquarters.

This Christmas, if you want to give a gift that keeps on giving— how about a pregnant cat?

On December 11, 1909, the first public showing of movies in color was achieved by running film through red and green screens. Viewers complained of headaches.

Peter's Constitutional Principle: Every American is endowed with certain inalienable rights—life, liberty, and a share of the national debt.

NATIONAL DING-A-LING DAY *December 12*

DECEMBER 12 is sponsored by the National Ding-a-Ling Club as National Ding-a-Ling Day to promote the idea that just because a person is a ding-a-ling doesn't mean he or she can't be a wonderful, friendly, intelligent, loving, responsible and desirable person.

There is only one thing I can do better than anyone else—read my own handwriting.

On December 12, 1792, Ludwig van Beethoven, aged 22, paid 19 cents for his first music lesson from Franz Joseph Haydn in Vienna.

I just got a great present for my brother-in-law—a leaky ant farm.

On December 12, 1955, the Ford Foundation announced a gift of half a billion dollars to the nation's private hospitals, colleges, and medical schools, the largest single philanthropic act in world history.

Peter's Delegation Principle: Anything worth doing is worth getting someone else to do.

FEAST OF SANTA LUCIA *December 13*

THE FEAST OF SANTA LUCIA, or Saint Lucy, an early Christian virgin and martyr, is an occasion for festivities in Italy and Scandinavia and those parts of the United States in which Swedish immigrants settled. Saint Lucy was martyred December 13, 304. Legends abound about her life. One says that she was eagerly sought in marriage by a nobleman who claimed he was haunted night and day by the beauty of her eyes. Such was her devotion to the religious life that she cut out her eyes and sent them to him on a plate and begged him henceforth to leave her alone. Her name is derived from the Latin *lux* or "light." She is honored as the patron saint of streetlamp lighters and those who suffer eye disease or imminent blindness. In medieval art, Lucy is depicted holding a torch or lamp or a plate on which lie two eyeballs.

Never put off until tomorrow what can be avoided altogether.

On December 13, 1927, Yehudi Menuhin, a ten-year-old child violinist made his very successful New York debut at a concert in Carnegie Hall. After the triumphant recital he was asked what he would like next. He said, "Some ice cream."

I never criticize the office party—anything that let's you eat, drink, and live it up on company time can't be all bad.

On December 13, 1928, George Gershwin's *An American in Paris* had its premiere performance by the New York Philharmonic.

Peter's Nostalgia Principle: The good old days were when time was marching on—instead of running out.

SAN FRANCISCO-TO-HONOLULU CABLE ANNIVERSARY

December 14

ON DECEMBER 14, 1902, the cable ship *Silverton* set out from San Francisco to lay the first cable from there to Honolulu. On January 1, 1903, the *Silverton* reached Honolulu and the cable was ready to transmit messages.

If you can keep your head while all about you are losing theirs—you probably don't know what's going on.

On December 14, 1936, the delightful play by Moss Hart and George S. Kaufman, *You Can't Take It with You*, opened for a long run at the Booth Theatre in New York.

This Christmas both the kids and my money sprouted wings.

On December 14, 1910, a gift of $10 million from Andrew Carnegie established The Carnegie Endowment for International Peace. The purpose of the new organization was to work toward international peace through research, publications, and other educational activities.

Peter's Academic Principle: If you can't understand it, name it.

ON DECEMBER 15, 1791, the first ten amendments to the U.S. Constitution, known as the Bill of Rights, became effective following ratification by Virginia. December 15, as Bill of Rights Day, has been made official by a number of Presidential Proclamations and since 1968 has been included in the Human Rights Week Proclamations.

Christmas sales confuse me. I don't know whether I'm honoring the birth of Christ or the store's inventory.

On December 15, 1791, the trustees of the University of Pennsylvania, at Philadelphia, elected James Wilson to the post of professor of law. This was the beginning of the first law school in the United States.

I am proud of our aluminum Christmas tree every time I hear the fire engine go by.

On December 15, 1890, Sitting Bull, chief of the Sioux Indians, was shot and killed in South Dakota following a skirmish with federal troops.

Peter's Tunnel-Vision Theory: We're all prejudiced because nobody can look in two directions at the same time.

ON DECEMBER 16, 1773, in protest against the British tax on tea, 7,000 people assembled at a town meeting in Boston. As evening approached about 50 men, dressed as Indians and yelling war cries, led the crowd to the wharves. They then boarded a British vessel at anchor in the harbor and broke open 342 chests of tea that were in the hold and threw the contents into the water.

Whatever goes wrong, there is always someone who knew it would.

On December 16, 1916, Grigori Rasputin, the mad monk who wielded a powerful influence over the Czar and Czarina of Russia, was lured to a Petrograd palace and poisoned. When this failed to kill him, he was stabbed to death and his body sunk beneath the ice of a local canal.

The Christmas tree lot reminded me that only God can make a tree—and only man can make a buck.

On December 16, 1905, *Variety*, a weekly periodical devoted to all phases of show business, was published for the first time by its founder, Sime Silverman. The first issue contained 16 pages and sold for 5 cents.

Peter's Law of Compensation: When my children lived at home I could never find my tools to fix things. Now that they have left, nothing gets broken.

ON DECEMBER 17, 1903, Orville and Wilbur Wright made the first successful airplane flights in history as they soared over the sand dunes near Kitty Hawk, North Carolina. The first flight with Orville at the controls lasted just 12 seconds. At 12 noon, Wilbur took off and managed to stay aloft for 59 seconds. Later, the Wright brothers recalled this historic morning: "The first flights with the power machine were made on December 17, 1903. Only five persons besides ourselves were present . . . . Although a general invitation had been extended to the people living within five or six miles, not many were willing to face the rigors of a cold December wind in order to see, as they no doubt thought, another flying machine not fly." Wright Brothers Day, in recognition of the first documented successful powered and controlled flight of an airplane, is established by Presidential Proclamation.

A man's best friend is his dogma.

On December 17, 1791, a traffic regulation in New York City established the first one-way street.

The department store Santa Claus suffered from water on the knee—several times a day.

On December 17, 1978, British women surveyed by a shirt manufacturer reported that a man with a slight paunch is preferable (34 percent) to a large paunch (31 percent) and definitely more interesting than no paunch (20 percent).

Peter's Notoriety Principle: It is possible to be involved in a spectacular, headline-making accident without any rehearsals whatsoever.

ON DECEMBER 18, 1865, slavery was abolished in the United States by the adoption of the Thirteenth Amendment to the Constitution, declared in effect as of this date by Secretary of State Seward: "Neither slavery nor involuntary servitude, except as a punishment for crime whereof the party shall have been legally convicted, shall exist within the United States, or any place subject to their jurisdiction."

He received his Christmas present late. He wanted a soldier suit when he was eight—ten years later he joined the army.

I told my kids what I wanted for Christmas—for them to hang up three things, stockings, mistletoe, and the phone.

Santa and Uncle Sam have a lot in common—they both leave goodies all over the world and end up holding the bag.

On December 18, 1936, the first giant panda to be imported into the United States arrived at San Francisco from China.

Peter's Routing Principle: In government bureaucracies difficult inquiries get passed to the lowest level of obscurity.

ON DECEMBER 18, 1958, at 3:15 P.M. (EDT) the United States satellite Atlas began the first radio-voice broadcast from space. It was a 58-word recorded Christmas greeting from President Dwight D. Eisenhower, including, ". . . to all mankind, America's wish for peace on earth and goodwill toward men everywhere."

He who quotes the learned sages will be known far and wide as a smartass.

On December 19, 1959, Walter Williams, 117 years old, the last surviving veteran of the Civil War, died in Houston, Texas. Williams served with the Confederate forces in the Texas Brigade.

Christmas is when you show goodwill to all living things by first cutting down a Christmas tree.

On December 19, 1732, Benjamin Franklin began publication of *Poor Richard's Almanack*, a series of booklets full of aphorisms and homely sayings.

Peter's Charity Principle: Don't give till it hurts. Give till it feels good.

LOUISIANA PURCHASE ANNIVERSARY

ON DECEMBER 20, 1803, in a ceremony in the heart of New Orleans, the flag of France was replaced by the flag of the United States, symbolizing the official transfer of the lands making up the Louisiana Purchase from French to American control. This purchase of more than a million square miles for a price of about $20 per square mile was one of the greatest real-estate deals in history.

Genius is 10 percent inspiration and 90 percent capital gains.

On December 20, 1928, Ethel Barrymore became the first living actress of the United States to have a theatre named after her when the Ethel Barrymore Theatre was opened in New York.

There's a perfect gift for the child who has everything—batteries.

December 20 is also called Mudd Day in remembrance of Dr. Samuel A. Mudd (born December 20, 1833) who was sentenced to life imprisonment for giving medical aid to John Wilkes Booth, fleeing assassin of Abraham Lincoln. Mudd was pardoned after serving four years.

Peter's Rule about Rules: Nobody ever breaks a rule until somebody makes one.

ALTHOUGH THEIR SHIP, the *Mayflower*, had reached Cape Cod on November 11, the Pilgrims first set foot on American soil at Plymouth, Massachusetts, on December 21, 1620. Forefathers' Day, observed mainly in New England, is in commemoration of this landing.

Don't worry if you waited till the last minute to buy your Christmas presents. So did the Three Wise Men.

On December 21, 1844, Charles Haworth and 27 poverty-stricken associates, established a store in Rochelle, England. This store, based on the idea of ownership by the customers, was the beginning of the cooperative movement.

A penny saved is ridiculous.

On December 21, 1937, the animated cartoon *Snow White and the Seven Dwarfs*, produced by Walt Disney and based on a Grimms' fairy tale, was shown in Los Angeles for the first time.

Peter's Theory of Reciprocal Inhibition of Fiscal Recall: Lending money to friends causes them to lose their memories.

NATIONAL FLASHLIGHT DAY *December 22*

THE PURPOSE OF this December 22 observation is to promote awareness of how flashlights play an important role in everyone's everyday life.

To us he's Rudolph the Red-Nosed Reindeer—to Dancer, Prancer, Donder, and Blitzen he's a wino.

Gilles de Laval, the model for the fairy-tale tyrant Bluebeard, was executed by strangulation on December 22, 1440. He had been a captain under Jeanne d'Arc and the richest man in France. He was an incredible libertine of depraved and criminal tastes who confessed to assault, torture, and murder of scores of children.

It's not the money, it's the principal and interest.

On December 22, 1886, Henry Woodfin Grady, editor of the *Atlanta Constitution*, introduced the phrase the "New South" in a speech before the members of the New England Club of New York City: "There is a New South, not through protests against the old, but because of new conditions, new adjustments, and, if you please, new ideas and aspirations."

Peter's Theory of Protective Coloration: Mailbags are colored gray so they won't show the dust.

ON DECEMBER 23, 1975, the Congress of the United States passed the Metric Conversion Act of 1975. This act declares that the International System of Units will be this country's eventual system of measurement and established the United States Metric Board with responsibility to plan, coordinate, and implement the nation's voluntary conversion to metric.

Each time we see a politician making a speech, we are reminded that Christmas is not the only time we see a turkey stuffed with chestnuts.

On December 23, 1732, English industrialist Richard Arkwright was born. By inventing the cotton-spinning frame he accelerated the Industrial Revolution.

The only thing I didn't like about office Christmas parties was having to look for a new job the next week.

On December 23, 1947, John Bardeen, Walter H. Brattain, and William Shockley invented the transistor.

Peter's Yuletide Principle: Christmas is the one day on which pasts and futures are of less interest than the presents.

DECEMBER 24 IS A FAMILY gift-giving occasion in many Christian countries. The customs of Christmas Eve and Day are an amalgam of the practices of many places and times. The custom of decorating a tree for the season comes from medieval German. The hangings of mistletoe comes from the Druids in England who at their festival of the solstice cut it from their most sacred tree, the oak, believing in its great healing powers. The Yule log comes from Scandinavia where the burning of a log on the lord's hearth was the main social event of the season. This arose from the ancient rite of winter solstice when huge fires were built.

If the Christmas story happened today the miracle would be the appearance of Three Wise Men.

On December 24, 1871, Verdi's spectacular opera *Aida* had its world premiere in Cairo, Egypt. The composer was commissioned to write the opera at the request of the khedive of Egypt as part of the festivities celebrating the opening of the Suez Canal.

On December 24, 1818, Franz Gruber of Oberndorf, Germany, composed the music for *Silent Night* to words by Josef Mohr. It was sung for the first time on Christmas Day.

Peter's Accumulation-of-Filth Principle: Cleaning anything involves making something else dirty, but anything can get dirty without something else getting clean.

THE DATE OF CHRISTMAS was not set until the time of Julius I, bishop of Rome from 337 to 352. Before that, Christians celebrated the birth of Christ at various times of the year. Some observed the first or sixth of January, some the twenty-ninth of March, near the Jewish Passover, and some September 29 about the time of the Feast of Tabernacles. In the early fourth century more and more places came to celebrate the nativity around the winter solstice. Julius made inquiries into the matter and according to what seemed the soundest traditions, chose December 25 as the date for Christmas.

If the Star of Bethlehem appeared in the sky today the U.S. Air Force would issue a bulletin claiming it was a weather balloon.

On December 25, 1875, a group of men prominent in the theatre, music, art, and literature, got together and founded the Lambs Club of New York.

Child looking at the bottoms of the boxes his Christmas toys came in: "Santa must have moved his workshop to Japan."

From 1659 to 1681, it was illegal to celebrate Christmas in Massachusetts.

Peter's Christmas Message: Even if it's warm today, have a cool Yule.

DECEMBER 26 IS ordinarily observed as Boxing Day unless it falls on a day that would not be a regular working day. It is a legal holiday in Canada, the United Kingdom (except Scotland) and many other countries. Formerly it was a day when Christmas gift boxes were regularly expected by apprentices, the postman, the lamplighter, the dustman, and all those functionaries who render service to the public at large. When Boxing Day falls on a Saturday or Sunday, the Monday immediately following may be proclaimed or observed as a public holiday.

Today is when you learn the true meaning of those famous words "batteries not included."

Christmas bills are the real mourning after.

On December 26, 1931, an enthusiastic audience was on hand at the Music Box Theatre in New York for the opening of George Gershwin's musical *Of Thee I Sing*. Besides being a smash hit, this show was the first musical to win a Pulitzer Prize for drama.

The bigger they are, the harder they maul.

On December 26, 1865, James Mason of Franklin, Massachusetts, was awarded a patent for his invention of a coffee percolator, the first such device in the United States.

Peter's Technological Principle: Automatic means if something goes wrong, you can't fix it.

SWEET ADELINE ANNIVERSARY

ON DECEMBER 27, 1903, "Sweet Adeline," the all-time favorite song with barbershop quartets, composed by Henry Armstrong to words written by Richard Gerard, was sung for the first time in New York City. The title for the song was suggested to the composers when they saw the name of the great operatic soprano, Adelina Patti, on a theatre marquee.

He who uses foul language is a rotten, dumb schmuck.

On December 27, 1900, Carrie Nation staged her first raid on a saloon as she marched into the bar at the Carey Hotel in Wichita, Kansas, and smashed all the liquor bottles in sight.

Hindsight is an exact science.

On December 27, 1932, Radio City Music Hall opened in New York City.

Peter's Activity Principle: Always consult your doctor before strenuous exercise. There's a chance he may advise against it.

ON DECEMBER 28, 1869, William Semple of Mount Vernon, Ohio, obtained a patent for ". . . the combination of rubber with other articles in any proportions adapted to the formation of an acceptable chewing gum."

A house divided against itself is a duplex.

On December 28, 1869, the Knights of Labor observed this day as Labor Day, the first such observance in American history.

Modern life is a mad dash through a chemical minefield.

Ask not for whom the bell tolls—and pay only the station-to-station rate.

On December 28, 1832, Vice President John C. Calhoun, who was in disagreement with President Jackson, resigned from office and filled a vacancy in the Senate caused by the resignation of Senator Robert Y. Hayne of South Carolina.

Peter's Diet Principle: If you are thin—don't eat fast. If you are fat—don't eat; fast.

ON DECEMBER 29, 1777, George Washington's troops at Valley Forge were saved from mutiny by the ingenuity of an army cook. Faced with hunger and cold the general pleaded with his chef to concoct a warming dish to raise the men's morale. The chef obtained a large quantity of tripe, some peppercorns, and vegetables. With these ingredients he invented Philadelphia Pepper Pot and nourished the soldiers while preventing a revolt.

The perfect festive season is a Christmas you'll never forget and a New Year's you'll never remember.

On December 29, 1848, President Polk and the staff of the Executive Mansion witnessed the installation of the first gas-lights in the White House.

On December 29, 1890, more than 200 American Indians—men, women, and children—were massacred by the U.S. Cavalry at Wounded Knee Creek, South Dakota. Government efforts to suppress a ceremonial religious practice, The Ghost Dance, which called for a messiah who would restore the bison to the plains, make the white men disappear, and bring back the old Indian way of life, had resulted in the death of Sitting Bull and culminated in the slaughter at Wounded Knee.

Peter's Theory of Bureaucratic Power: This country belongs to the people who inhibit it.

GADSDEN PURCHASE DAY   *December 30*

ON DECEMBER 30, 1853, as the result of negotiations between Mexico and the United States minister to that nation, James Gadsden, the United States acquired some 45,000 square miles of land south of the Gila River for a purchase price of $10 million. The acreage included in this so-called Gadsden Purchase was incorporated in what is now the southern portions of Arizona and New Mexico.

Give a man enough rope—and he'll fill the house with plants in funny-looking macrame hangers.

Of the two four-word greetings, "This is a stickup" and "Have a nice day," the former is the most sincere.

December 30 commemorates a miracle at sea. On May 15, 1834, the British ship *Resolute* was abandoned in the treacherous ice near Melville Island. Captain Buddington of the American whaler *George Henry* found the Resolute 474 days later, adrift near Cape Mercy. The ship had miraculously made the 1,000-mile trip through the Barrow Straits, Lancaster Sound, and Baffin Bay. By an act of Congress, on December 30, 1856, the ship was given back to England and the Union Jack was once again hoisted on the *Resolute*.

Peter's Patriotic Principle: One should love one's country intelligently while avoiding the extremes of boastful superiority or self-contempt.

RINGING OUT THE OLD YEAR and ringing in the new at the stroke of twelve midnight on December 31, by making noise with horns and rattles followed by singing "Auld Lang Syne," has become the traditional New Year's Eve celebration. This grew out of the English and Scottish Hogmanay, an end-of-the-year celebration in which children go from house to house ringing doorbells.

New Year's resolutions prohibiting a person from doing what he or she would like to do are bound to fail, whereas resolutions forcing one to do what he or she likes to do will be successful.

On December 31, 1776, to curb the threat of runaway inflation, the legislature of Rhode Island fixed ceilings on some wages and commodity prices. The daily wages of carpenters were not to exceed 70 cents and those of tailors were set at 42 cents. Barbers were prohibited from charging more than 3.5 cents for a shave. Ceiling prices on turkey were established at 9 cents a pound, on milk at 9 cents a gallon, on rum at 63 cents a gallon. Taverns were forbidden to charge travelers more than 5 cents for a night's lodging.

On New Year's Eve an old man leaves and a newborn babe enters, and those in the middle stay and pay all year.

On December 31, 1879, a crowd of New Year's Eve revelers assembled at Menlo Park, New Jersey, to attend the first public demonstration of lighting with Thomas Edison's new incandescent lamp.

Peter's New Year Toast: May your troubles last as long as your New Year's resolutions.

ALPHABETICAL INDEX OF DAYS

GI Joe Day   June 17
Gibbon Inspiration Day   October 15
Gideon Sundback Day   April 29
Goat Mother Day   July 9
Goddard Day   March 16
Golden Spike Day   May 10
Gold Rush Day   January 24
Good Bear Day   October 27
Good Society Day   September 2
Go West, Young Man Day   July 13
Grand Canyon Day   February 26
Grandmother Achievement Day
   February 11
Grange Day   December 4
Gregorian Calendar Day   February 24
Greenwich Observatory Day   August 10
Greetings from Space Day   December 19
Groundhog Day   February 2
Guy Fawkes Day   November 5

Halloween   October 31
Hawaii Admission Day   August 21
Holy Experiment Day   March 4
Horse Kicks Teacher Day   September 28
Horse Versus Machine Day   August 25
Human Rights Day   December 10

Ice-Cream Cone Day   July 23
Ides of March   March 15
Illinois Day   February 3
Independence Day   July 4
Insulin Day   April 15
International Literacy Day   September 8
International Picnic Day   June 18
International Women's Day   March 8

Jackson Day   January 8
James H. Meredith Day   September 24
Jazz at the Met Day   January 18
Jesse Owens' Day   August 9
Johnny Appleseed Day   March 11
John Glenn Day   February 20
John Wilmot Day   July 26
Jumping Frog Jubilee   May 19

King Christian Resistance Day   October 7
King Tut's Discovery Day   November 29
Klondike Gold Rush   August 16

Lady Godiva Day   May 31
Lame Duck Amendment Day   February 6
Leap Year Day   February 29
Leif Ericson Day   October 9
Library of Congress Day   April 24
Life Insurance Founder's Day   January 11
Lindbergh Day   May 21
Lizzie Borden Acquittal Day   June 20
Long Distance Day   March 27
Lost Day   September 3
Louisiana Purchase Anniversary
   December 20
Lucy Stone's Birthday   August 13

Manhattan Purchase Day   May 4
Man in Space Day   April 12
Marconi Day   April 25
Mark Hopkins Day   February 4
Mark Twain Day   June 9
Martians Invade New Jersey Day
   October 30
Martin Luther King, Jr.'s Birthday
   January 15
May Day   May 1
Mayflower Departure Day   September 16
Medical Registration Day   September 26
Melba Toast Day   March 23
Metric Conversion Day   December 23
Mickey Mouse Birthday   November 18
Midair Gas-Up Day   June 27
Mississippi River Discovery Day   May 8
Model T Ford Day   October 1
Monkeys in Space Day   May 28
Monroe Doctrine Day   December 2
Moon Day   July 20
Most Famous Mutiny Day   April 28
Motion Picture Day   April 21
Mount Kennedy Summit Day   March 24

National Anthem Day   March 3

National Aviation Day   August 19
National Cheer Up the Lonely Day   July 11
National Ding-a-ling Day   December 12
National Flashlight Day   December 22
National Freedom Day   February 1
National Handwriting Day   January 23
National Maritime Day   May 22
National Neighborhood Day   September 11
National Non-Parent Day   August 1
National Pig Day   March 1
National Printing Ink Day   January 13
National Research Council Anniversary
   September 20
Newspaper Carrier Day   September 4
New Year's Day   January 1
New Year's Eve   December 31
New York Times Birthday   September 18
No Beard Day   October 19
No Bull Peace Prize Day   November 4
No Niagara Falls Day   March 29
Norma Currie Day   May 30

Oatmeal Diet Day   October 29
Old Maid's Day   June 4
Old Man's Day   October 2
Old People's Day   September 15
Old Stuff Day   March 2
One Cent Day   April 2
Orangemen's Day   July 12

Painless Dentistry Day   September 30
Painless Surgery Day   October 16
Palace Theatre Day   March 25
Panama Canal Day   January 7
Pan American Day   April 14
Paper Money Day   March 10
Parachute Fallout Day   October 22
Passport Photo Day   November 20
Patron Saint of Dentists Day   February 9
Paul Revere's Day   April 18
Peace Officers Memorial Day   May 15
Pepper Pot Day   December 29
Perils of Pauline Day   April 4
Phonograph Day   February 19
Pictures Move and Talk Day   October 6

Pikes Peak Discovery Day   November 15
Pins and Needles Day   November 27
Player Piano Day   September 6
Pocahontas Wedding Day   April 5
Pony Express Day   April 3
Positive Thinking Day   September 13
President Rating Day   July 29
President's House Cornerstone Day
   October 13
Prohibition Repeal Day   December 5
PTA Founders Day   February 17

Rabbit Celebrity Day   November 1
Radium Day   April 20
Refrigeration Day   May 6
Revolving Door Day   August 7
Robert's Rules Day   May 2
Roosevelt Survival Day   October 14

Saint Andrew's Day   November 30
Saint Charles's Day   January 30
Saint Crispin's Day   October 25
Saint Genevieve Feast Day   January 3
Saint George's Feast Day   April 23
St. Lawrence Seaway Day   June 26
Saint Nicholas's Day   December 6
Saint Patrick's Day   March 17
Saint Scholastica's Day   February 10
Saint Swithin's Day   July 15
Salvation Army Day   July 5
Samuel Morse Day   May 24
Sandwich Day   November 3
San Francisco-to-Honolulu Cable Anniversary
   December 14
Saturday Night Massacre Anniversary
   October 20
Saxophone Liberation Day   July 31
Scrubwomen Tea Party Day   June 16
Sea-to-Shining-Sea Anniversary
   November 7
Serendipity Day   January 28
Sheik Day   November 13
Singing Telegram Day   July 28
Slavery Abolition Day   December 18
Smallpox Vaccination Day   May 14

SOS Day **November 22**

Space Age Day **October 4**

SPCA Day **April 10**

Spinach Festival Day **March 26**

Spooner's Day **July 22**

Stanley Meets Livingstone Anniversary
  November 10

Statia and America Day **November 16**

Street Letter Box Day **August 2**

Suez Canal Anniversary **November 17**

Susan B. Anthony Day **February 15**

Swallows Return to Capistrano Day
  March 19

Swap Ideas Day **September 10**

Sweet Adeline Anniversary **December 27**

Talking Picture Day **July 6**

Taxpayer Revolt Day **June 6**

Technicolor Day **January 19**

Television News Day **February 16**

Telstar 2 Launch Day **May 7**

Texas Settlement Day **February 18**

Thanksgiving Proclamation Day **October 3**

This Is the Place Anniversary **July 24**

Ticker Tape Parade Day **June 13**

Tower of Pisa Day **February 27**

Truman Beats the Pollsters Day
  November 2

Turkey Day **January 26**

Tuxedo Debut Day **October 10**

Twelfth Day **January 6**

Twentieth Century Technological
  Vulnerability Day **November 9**

Typewriter Day **June 23**

Typewriter Ribbon Day **September 14**

Uncle Sam Day **March 13**

Union Victory Day **April 9**

United American Day **November 6**

United Nations Day **October 24**

U.S. Coast Guard Day **August 4**

U.S. Constitution Ratification Day **June 21**

United States Day **September 9**

United States Dollar Day **August 8**

United States Hottest Day **July 10**

Valentine's Day **February 14**

Van Cliburn Day **April 13**

Vanderbilt Cup Day **October 8**

Vaudeville Day **February 23**

Vernal Equinox Day **March 20**

Verrazano Day **April 17**

Veterans Day **November 11**

Vietnam Cease-Fire Day **January 27**

Virginia Dare Day **August 18**

Washing Improvement Day **March 28**

Washington's Birthday **February 22**

W. C. Fields Day **January 29**

Weatherman's Day **February 5**

Western Movie Day **May 17**

Will Rogers Refusal Day **June 28**

Winter Flowers Day **December 8**

Woman Suffrage Planning Day
  November 24

Women's Equality Day **August 26**

Women's Rights Day **July 19**

World Environment Day **June 5**

World Goodwill Day **May 18**

World Health Day **April 7**

World Hello Day **November 21**

World Sauntering Day **August 28**

World Series Broadcast Day **October 5**

Wright Brothers Day **December 17**

Wrong Way Corrigan Day **July 17**

Xenophobe Understanding Day
  September 29

Yankee Yacht Victory Day **August 22**

Zeppelin Passenger Day **June 22**